Don't Worry:

How to Beat
the Seven Anxieties of Life

D0542153

Douglas Miller

BARNET LIBRARIES	
Bertrams	22.02.07
152.46	£9.99

PEARSON

Prentice Hall

LIFE

Pearson Education Limited
Edinburgh Gate
Harlow
Essex CM20 2JE
England

First published 2007

ISBN 978-0-2737-1269-5

Commissioning Editor: Emma Shackleton
Project Editor: Jeanette Payne
Designer: Kevin O'Connor
Senior Production Controller: Man Fai Lau

Printed and bound by Henry Ling, UK

The Publisher's policy is to use paper manufactured from sustainable forests.

CONTENTS

THE AUTHOR

Douglas Miller is a practical psychologist, writer and trainer specializing in positive thinking, motivation, anxiety/stress, creativity and leadership. He is based in London and Montpellier, France. His work takes him all over Europe (including Kosovo, Georgia and Macedonia) for international organizations including the United Nations and the Organization for Security and Co-operation in Europe (OSCE) as well as many private and public-sector organizations in the UK. Readers can contact him on doug@dougmiller.demon.co.uk.

Other books by the author

Positive Thinking, Positive Action
Make Your Own Good Fortune

PREFACE

'Ninety per cent of what we worry about never happens, yet we worry and worry. What a horrible way to go through life! What a horrible thing to do to your colon!'

Leo Buscaglia,
author of *Living, Loving and Learning*

Will the trains be running? Am I pregnant? What happens if I don't get the upgrade? What would I do if I fell ill? I *am* ill – what does the future hold? Can I feed my family? How many are likely to be made redundant? When will the rain come? When will the rain stop? Should I change jobs? Windows, Linux or OS X? What's everyone going to be wearing next summer? Do I have to spend another day with my boss? Am I getting old? What's happened to my marriage? What about me? What happens if the drains block? Is this a good place to leave the car? Could anyone break into the house? Are my children going to have a happy life? What is the rest of my life going to be like? How much longer can I work with that idiot? Will this empty feeling last forever? Why does life seem like one big struggle? Why is everyone having more sex than me? MMR or single jab? Which ISP? Why am I eating so much? What will my new boss be like? Where am I going? What's the traffic going to be like on the way to IKEA? What happens when I retire? How many cars do I need?

Well, if you weren't actually feeling anxious when you picked up this book I am sorry to have reminded you of some of the anxieties you may currently 'own'! Of course, some of the questions on that list relate to critical life issues – worries about feeding the family and the reality of serious illness are issues that will create an almost uncontrollable anxiety in most, if not all, of us.

A second list of questions might include the things that create anxiety in many, but fortunately not all, of us. Some of the more existential 'Why am I here?' type questions would fit into this new list. So, too, would the fear of a bad boss, or the fear of one's own inadequacy in work or non-work activities.

In a third category we could place issues that relate to life in consumerist societies – ones that might amuse readers from apparently less 'wealthy' parts of the world, but which create serious problems for those who suffer from anxieties produced by the society of which they are a part. Issues such as 'being in fashion' and owning the next 'must-have' gadget create considerable anxiety for teenagers, and these pressures to conform to 'populist tendencies' often permeate into full adulthood.

Even at this early stage of the book you may find it useful to think about your own anxieties. I assume you have picked up the book because you have some awareness of them or because you currently feel anxious but are not quite sure why. Perhaps the opening paragraph has stimulated you to consider some factors that you may have dismissed previously, or at least left unchallenged. Why not give some thought now as to what the causes of your current anxieties are or might be?

Walking into emptiness

In western democracies, anxiety has become one of the critical issues of our time. Our lives have become easier, longer and healthier, and our opportunities have never been greater or more diverse. And yet, at the same time, more of us describe ourselves as depressed, stressed or in some way disconnected than ever before – perhaps we recognize that life could be 'better' for us but we are not quite sure why. In the last decade, many studies have been done that seem to show that people were less anxious and more content in a previous age than they are now. And this is a phenomenon that seems to be shared across the UK, USA, continental Europe and countries such as Australia and Japan.

These studies can and should be challenged. Many hark back to a post-Second World War golden age, but it is worth remembering that, at that time, many people were experiencing a huge sense of post-war optimism (even with the cold war threat) and were able to buy things like vacuum cleaners, fridges and televisions for the first time. Nowadays, the decisions are about what kind of vacuum cleaner to buy rather than whether we should own one at all. It surely adds to our anxieties to be told that others were happier than us in times gone by, particularly when it may not be true.

It is a better use of our time to look at why it is that many of us seem to move between a position of wistful melancholia and a subtle but noticeable sense of something 'missing', punctuating this with unnatural instant highs to get through the next day, week or year. This may be a stereotypical existence, but many wouldn't deny that they have experienced this feeling for significant periods of their life even when, on the surface, everything seems fine. France, for example, often said to be the cradle of high quality of life, has an alarmingly high number of people who take antidepressants – four times the European average, according to some statistics. While this may be due in part to an over-eagerness for French doctors and psychiatrists to prescribe antidepressants and tranquillizers (and an over-reliance on the old Freudian method of couch-and-notepad psychiatry), the fact is that the patient still has to go to the doctor and identify himself or herself as being anxious or unhappy.

A strong education system and terrific healthcare do not necessarily generate 'happiness' – and the evidence in France, and indeed in other countries with top-level state healthcare, is that there is a belief that a leg-up to a happier, less anxious state can be obtained from the doctor's surgery rather than from the self. Great healthcare certainly makes the business of living easier, but does easy living mean happy living? Many would say 'no'. It is as though we know that a part of us is missing amidst all of this comfort. The body is well fed, watered and looked after, but the spirit remains 'hungry'. And the 'spirit' is one of the strongest personal resources available to us to combat anxiety.

Before we seek to eliminate anxiety completely we should remember that mild anxiety can sharpen our mental faculties. But most of us get an intuitive feel when something doesn't seem right in our current circumstances – most noticeably when the anxiety begins to have a negative effect on our well-being. We often choose to ignore the signs.

About this book

This is a book that aims to present many of the classic causes of anxiety in the modern world and to show some ways of overcoming them. I have focused on seven primary causes – one per chapter.

A word on what this book is not. It is not a book designed to help those who have a medical condition related to anxiety or stress. I am not qualified to diagnose medical conditions or to recommend treatments – although like many readers I can readily recognize many of the physical, psychological and behavioural symptoms at a superficial level. And, in particular, it is not a book aimed at those who believe they may be suffering from clinical depression or who have suicidal tendencies.

It is a book that showcases some of the challenges that we meet in everyday living and how we can begin not just to survive but also to thrive in pressurized, anxiety-ridden cultures. These are cultures that are not limited only to the obvious ones like the USA, UK, Australia or Western Europe. Places such as Bangalore in India, Shanghai in China, São Paolo in Brazil and parts of the former Soviet Union are accelerating so fast economically and socially that the lifestyles of the growing economic elites there are not so far removed from those in the traditional economic powerhouses. With the economic explosion in significant parts of India, China, Brazil and Russia we are likely to see a dramatic shift in priorities in those places which are benefiting from the new prosperity and the new anxieties that these economic changes will bring to them.

It seems crazy, doesn't it? Just as a massive new group of people moves out of thousands of years of poverty, with all the attendant stresses and anxieties that this will have bought, we then suggest that they will have a whole raft of new ones to overcome. Certainly out of the rough comes the not quite smooth, but it may well be, as I make clear in this book, that some (and only some) of the 'jagged edges' in more prosperous societies are false anxieties born of the need to fill some kind of emotional vacuum in our life. There are of course other anxieties that are very real.

INTRODUCTION

What is anxiety?

Before we examine the seven anxieties, it may be useful to say what 'anxiety' is and how it relates to its near cousin 'stress'. Anxiety is a behaviour that is learned through experience and conditioning and one that relates to our perception of the future. That future can be the next minute, the next hour, day, week, year or the rest of your life. Anxiety can be said to be the anticipation of an event or chain of events that generates a range of emotions from mild apprehension through to fear, whether the basis for that apprehension or fear is groundless or a very realistic appraisal of what could happen.

Stress is a condition; an adverse reaction to current pressures that relates to our current circumstances. Anxiety can be therefore a cause of stress, but stress can also be a cause of anxiety. In some sections of the book – particularly the chapter on the workplace – the two are interchangeable. The person who is stressed because of work may well be anxious about the work itself and the damage that it is doing to them.

I should also point out that a degree of anxiety is good for us – it helps us to perform. Anxiety has come about as a valuable mechanism in helping us to protect ourselves through evolution. Imagine if we had felt no sense of danger in the presence of a sabre-tooth tiger! So we can and should learn to value a degree of anxiety as a vital defence mechanism. But we should note that, while this flight response provides protection, it is not always the best reaction. We learnt this when we saw that at times we had to fight. Perhaps we needed to protect and defend our families and communities or maybe we just saw the next meal in front of us.

In the world of the modern *Homo sapiens* this fight response has evolved into something less aggressive but equally valuable when it comes to protecting ourselves. We all need pressure in varying amounts. Pressure can help us to give the very best of ourselves – sometimes well beyond the level of which we thought we were capable. Where that pressure becomes too much, to the point where we suffer an adverse reaction, then we become stressed. In the same way, being anxious can allow us to respond positively to the potentially troublesome event or circumstance we see ahead of us.

So a degree of anxiety can be good for us. But where that anxiety generates a response that is totally inappropriate to the situation, or where our personal well-being is diminished, then the physical, psychological and behavioural symptoms will be the same, or similar to those we get when we are stressed. Being anxious about the future can make us stressed in the present.

Anxiety can manifest itself, for example, in teenagers who, living in an age of strong peer pressure, may be 'anxious' because they don't have the right kind of mobile phone. It is curious at a time when we are at our most rebellious and newly independent that we often seek also to conform and to be part of a group. We can all sit in judgement at this apparently ludicrous cause of teenage angst. But remember, they will be sitting in judgement of our ludicrous-to-them anxieties too. I recall talking about music to the 14-year-old cousin of a friend of mine. When I challenged his choice of music ('death metal' as I recall), he said, 'All adults seem to listen to is music about being in love, love that has been lost, or love that you are looking for.' Probably very true!

The causes of anxiety

Life for all of us contains a number of jagged edges along a path we hope will be as smooth as possible, although it would be an extremely boring life if the path was a completely flat one. Many of the jagged edges can be seen as the primary causes of anxiety in us.

When I find myself asking groups about the causes of anxiety they are nearly always able to produce an extensive list, often based on personal experiences.

In the seven chapters of this book we highlight some of the primary causes of anxiety, from those that are underlying, such as searching for the meaning of life, through to the most easily recognizable, for example, those we experience in the workplace. A summary of the seven chapters follows.

Knowing yourself: Who am I?

Much modern thinking in the world of popular psychology asks us, rightly, to consider our own strengths and weaknesses and this takes us into the realm of knowing and understanding what you are truly capable of on a deeper level. Anxiety often comes from our perceiving that we do not have the psychological strengths and capabilities that we actually do. Self-perception frequently does not tie in with reality. This misalignment can leave us bereft of personal identity and believing that we cannot deal with realities.

While this chapter requires a degree of self-analysis, a key tenet is not to become so self-absorbed in it that we (a) become paralyzed by it or (b) try to become someone we are never likely to be.

In this chapter I suggest five simple exercises to help you to understand your own strengths and vulnerabilities. Your strengths are the things to celebrate but, as we become anxious, we lay emphasis on our weaknesses – real or imagined.

The meaning of life: What am I here for?

I was recently talking about the planets and the solar system with my six-year-old daughter. We started to discuss the 'Big Bang' theory and I tried, with my minimalist scientific knowledge, to explain how a lump of 'something' very small exploded and created the universe. Easy. But as we were having this conversation I found myself asking the obvious existentialist question: if the creation of what we know is so brutally scientific, and the creation of life almost an accidental

3

by-product of this, what am I here for? And the bigger question – 'Am I here for anything at all?' There may well be no bigger.

Organized religion often provides answers to those questions, but with the decline in the number of people who believe in a god or a higher being, the subject has moved way beyond the conjecture of 1960s hippy communes, and has become a conscious source of anxiety for many of us. Many of us need to feel a purpose in our life and become anxious if we do not find one. In this chapter we suggest ten ways in which we can discover meaning across a number of situations.

Consuming: Why do I need all this stuff?

The psychologist Abraham Maslow stated that the need to have food, water and shelter were needs that had to be satisfied before we would consider the option of graduating to a higher set of needs, such as the need for love and belonging, self-esteem, status and self-actualization. Although this 'Hierarchy of Needs' theory contains huge holes, the idea that we have needs beyond the most basic ones is very sound. But in post-industrial societies the non-basic needs are often met by the desire to consume to prove our worthiness in these areas. In an emotionally empty life, status, for example, can be conferred on us, or so we believe, because we have a great car or a big house. Self-actualization may involve the anticipation of massive wealth, rather than the vision of meaningful achievement.

We convince ourselves that the fulfilling of these needs through possession and consumption can be satisfied only by wanting and owning more. The emotional vacuum remains unfilled because it cannot be filled, except in the shortest of short terms, by 'stuff'. How can we learn to question and challenge our need to consume? How can we remove the anxiety around not having enough 'stuff'?

Relationships: How can they be stronger?

In this chapter we view strong relationships like a healthy tree – something that grows over time, suffers the vagaries of the weather and the seasons (relationships are never smooth), cross-pollinates frequently (good relationships are based on mutual benefit) and which often fruits and, or, lays seeds (children in the case of marriage and love). But good relationships have their basis in a number of learned emotional skills that can build and strengthen them.

Work: Why has it become my life?

When I do workshops on stress and anxiety, it is striking how many participants divide the causes up into 'work' and 'non-work' – such is the pervasive nature of work in our life. A recent study of the key 'pressure points' at work showed that the top ten anxiety and stress-inducing factors were as follows:

1 Constant interruptions
2 Time pressure
3 Poor internal communication
4 Lack of support
5 Poor senior management
6 Too many internal meetings
7 Office politics
8 Handling change
9 Securing the right information
10 Keeping up with emails

The anticipation of many of these – lack of time and dealing with predicted change (whether real or imagined), for example – makes us feel anxious about work. Sometimes even the very thought of going to work, as we see from several case studies in this and other chapters, makes us apprehensive. As we know from several high-profile court cases, the physical and psychological effects can be dramatic. The issues we explore here in this chapter relate to the smarter working practices that will help us thrive in what may be a hostile environment.

Time: Where did it go?

This is perhaps the most prominent of the 'false' anxieties. It is an irony that, at a time when we live longer than we ever have, and where it is

5

predicted that the current generation being born will live well beyond the age of 100, we seem to be in such a hurry. We have allowed ourselves to run at somebody else's pace, at a speed we do not feel comfortable with and where we inherit the time anxieties passed on to us by others. Most of it is so unnecessary and indeed the need to monitor time closely is a relatively modern phenomenon.

The future: What does it hold?

I contend that what most of us seek is happiness in our lives, although we are often confused or misguided about what it is that will bring us that happiness. Those confusions are often, as we see elsewhere in the book, the causes of anxiety – for example, the need to over-consume. The western world is sensing a decline in happiness, with governments seeking to have a major role in our future happiness. But really we cannot rely on governments to do this for us. If they succeed it may take 50 years. What can I do to make me happier in the future?

Sail the seven 'C's

As you read this book it will help to have in your mind what I believe are the seven strengths of the person who is able to deal with anxiety. Indeed I will regularly refer to, and remind you, of these core strengths as we go through the book. You may say that you don't have these strengths. But in truth we all own all of them because they form part of the fabric of what makes us human, and the most intelligent species our small planet has ever known. The key is learning to access them when we need to.

1   CHOICE

The one true freedom, which cannot be denied to any of us, is that we can always, no matter what the situation, choose the attitude we apply to that situation or to our circumstances. We can choose a positive one if we wish to. In the context of this book choice will come in two forms.

The first comes from using anxiety as a way to think positively. If we are able to consider what it is that is making us anxious, we then have a choice of paths to follow. The first path is the one where we choose a positive, proactive response to the perceived cause of our anxiety. This gives us the best chance of using our anxiety to positive ends. Or we can go for the second path, which is to 'hide away' and hope the problem will disappear (which it usually won't), or the third path, in which we are unable to get a degree of control and the anxiety gets worse.

In its second form we find ourselves in a challenging situation but we find it hard to see a way ahead. As we see later in this book, there are some wonderful examples of people who made it through by choosing to adopt a positive attitude.

2 CONTROL

There is a cliché that says, 'You cannot worry about what you cannot control'. This, although often tough to action, is completely true. The challenge, when combating anxiety, is to assess what you can control, act accordingly, and ignore what you cannot.

When things don't go quite right for us we often get locked into a mindset that seeks to understand why they didn't happen the way we planned. This is a good thing. It can help us identify what we need to work on to get it right next time. However, it can stifle us if we choose to reflect on circumstances beyond our control. We can ask endless 'Why?' questions and not get nearer to an answer. In the meantime we are not moving forward.

We have all met 'control freaks', who seek to plan meticulously every aspect of their lives (and sometimes ours too!). They, of course, fear loss of control more than most of us, which explains their actions. But in truth, trying to get control over things beyond our control, or where the effort to get control actually damages our physical and mental health, does not promote the necessary balance between control and freedom.

3 CAPABILITY

The only part of the world we can be certain of improving is our own world. However, we dramatically underestimate what it is we are capable of, and this underestimation can lead to a crippling loss of confidence, self-esteem and a whole host of other social skills. As we get older we tend to reflect on our lives and wonder if the things we did, or more importantly chose not to do, were a true reflection of our own capability. It can be debilitating, and a cause of subtle, creeping anxiety, to recognize that you are not living a life that is a reflection of the best bits of 'you'.

We all share the ability to work with our anxieties to positive effect. But, more significantly, we have the capability to come through some of the toughest, most challenging situations, as some of the case studies and stories in this book will show. If you are very anxious now it can be easy to believe that you are staring at a blacked-out window. But there is always a chink of light fighting to get through.

Sometimes we need help in opening the window to let more light in, but the smallest step begins with the willingness to believe that things can get better, and that it will be our personal psychological strengths that will make that happen. Every reader of this book has that capability.

4 COLLABORATION

In tough times, do not be afraid to share your vulnerabilities with those who can help you. And be prepared to let others share theirs with you too. In admitting anxiety to others, we feel sometimes that we may be showing weakness. We fear 'losing face'. The traditional argument said that to suppress one's feelings, or to fail to share them, was in some way an admirable personality trait – a test of psychological strength. But there is really nothing strong about hiding anxiety, or indeed stress.

Collaboration is about being unafraid to seek the help of others – whether those closest to us, or those who possess the appropriate professional skills. But do also recognize that there should be some balance here. A problem shared is helpful, but there's nothing more frustrating than the person who constantly shares their anxieties, while never seeming to do anything to help themselves. To talk is only one half of the equation. The other is to act, and that action can come only from you.

5 CONFIDENCE

Recognize the achievements in your life so far for what they are. But recognize, too, that the failures were a necessary precondition for those achievements. Don't beat yourself up over what didn't work. Champion what did.

While underestimating our capability is one way in which we limit our confidence, there are many others. Over-reflecting on our perceived failures, taking knock-backs at school, and being surrounded by the brash exteriors of others, all contribute as well.

There are many ways in which confidence can express itself. You may not wear your personality on your sleeve but this does not mean that you don't have what it takes to succeed at whatever it is you want to do.

6 COMMUNITY

When we feel anxious, we become inclined to give up the very things that can provide the escape route to a more balanced, fulfilling future. Reflecting our thoughts and stimulations back on to ourselves can blind us to the beauty of the real world – things that can provide essential perspective when we are going through personally challenging times. The importance of building 'community' into our lives is that it steers us away from too much self-reflection and back to things beyond the 'self'.

This allows us to re-engage with life, nature, friends, activities and hobbies – things that 'oxygenate' our lives. This 'oxygenation' is beneficial as it enhances our lives with a greater level of stimulation, which is essential when it comes to dealing with anxieties that stem from a lack of personal enrichment. Being able to remove the emphasis from yourself and use it as a positive way to combat current anxiety is an important counterweight to paralyzing self-analysis.

7 CONTRIBUTION

It is often said by people who lived through the Second World War that being able to see a direct correlation between what they did and its end result made them feel fulfilled, and gave them a powerful sense of having made a valuable contribution. Perhaps, these days, we have to search a little harder for evidence that we have an impact and to find a vocation that gives us a sense of value and fulfilment.

Having this feeling of fulfilment in our lives is critical as it removes those superfluous anxieties that would otherwise fill the void. If you don't feel fulfilled in your job (and you should not underestimate the contribution you make here), you need to seek it elsewhere – in things you do beyond the workplace.

If we believe that what we contribute is of little value, and we perceive that we have a lack of status, it can cause long-lasting anxiety and damage to self-esteem. But in these circumstances, it is useful to take stock and think about just how many people rely on you and what you do. Remember – we are all valuable.

So we begin the book's journey with you and your world. It is a journey that doesn't stop until the end of the book. But it is a journey that shows that, with some practical steps, we can learn both to combat anxiety and, when it suits us, thrive on it. The seven 'C's provide crucial mindsets that will help us along the way.

KNOWING YOURSELF:

Who am I?

'I have come to the conclusion that we can only really know ourselves through close observation; unless we catch our own reactions as they happen we can easily remain in ignorance of how we actually operate. It's a special sort of self-observation, that awareness that catches you as you're doing it, or just after.'

Chris Carling,
Communication expert, mediator and coach

Part One – Five exercises to help you get to know yourself

We tend to behave in the way we think we are – even if that is not a reflection of the real person. Believing, for example, that you are not creative is likely to lead you along a career path that does not emphasize creativity, although creativity can exist in any job. Some of us see ourselves as shy introverts, not recognizing that it is our fear of 'failing' in social situations that is paralyzing the social, more extrovert side of us. This is why alcohol is used as a social lubricant. It superficially takes away the fear of 'showing ourselves up' or 'saying the wrong thing'. Believing ourselves to be poor at public speaking can lead us to create the very circumstances we were fearful of, whereas, if we understand that we can be good, and use the anxiety to positive effect, we could actually surprise ourselves.

To help in the journey into knowing ourselves a little better, we start with a series of exercises that will help us to build a bigger and more accurate picture. But these, while useful, will go only so far in helping us to understand our own anxieties and emotional responses.

The next step, which we shall explore in this book, is to use those natural, emotional responses in positive ways.

Exercise 1: The four quadrants

This is an exercise used regularly by practitioners to help us understand how anxiety manifests itself in us. Those reactions will be subtly different in all of us because in the same way that a rope will break at its weakest point, anxiety, if we choose to ignore it, will eat away at our most vulnerable points.

EXERCISE

In this exercise (see opposite) there are four quadrants, which cover the symptoms of anxiety in four key areas: physical, psychological, behavioural and emotional. Your task is to circle those symptoms that you recognize in yourself. Do not circle too many – particularly in the 'physical' quadrant (most of us have one or two physical symptoms that shout loudest at us). You may find that a useful way to approach this is to think of a situation that has made you anxious in the recent past, and to think how that affected you in the four areas.

When presented with a list as comprehensive as this we can instantly recognize that we have suffered some of these symptoms, and may even be doing so at the moment. The value of this quick exercise is to help you to think a little more deeply about the 'anxiety' (and, indeed, stress) signals your mind and body sends out – an 'early warning system', if you like. When you recognize these signals you can, as many do, choose to ignore the signs and just carry on regardless. Sometimes that is fine because the causes of anxiety disappear. However, at other times they will not disappear just because you have chosen to ignore them, with the result that things get worse.

At other times the symptoms creep up on us more subtly. Either way, this is the point at which we should utilize the first of those valuable seven 'C's – CHOICE – and make a positive response when the warning signs are starting to show. I know myself that the weakest part of my body is my stomach, and that when I have

Physical symptoms

- Heart/chest: racing, palpitations, skipping a beat, raised blood pressure, tighter chest, irregular breathing
- Head: headaches/migraine, hot flushes/blushing, hair loss, head swirls/dizziness
- Skin: rashes, swellings, sweating
- Back: aches, pains
- Stomach: aching, regular toilet visits, over/under-eating
- Overall physicality: muscle fatigue, 'tinglings', proneness to colds, longer recovery from minor illnesses such as colds, upset stomach, tiredness

Psychological symptoms

- Fear of the future – feeling that the worst is going to happen
- Fear of being afraid – which makes you even more fearful
- Thoughts 'all over the place'
- Avoidance of challenging situations
- Lack of motivation or self-worth
- Low self-esteem/self-confidence
- Struggle to concentrate because of preoccupation with something else
- Trouble sleeping
- Memory loss
- Feeling of loss of control
- Detachment
- Inferiority complex

Emotional symptoms

- Highly sensitive
- Tearful/crying
- Inappropriate emotion for the situation
- Apprehension
- Depression
- Panic attacks
- Mood swings
- Melancholia/sadness
- Nervousness/unease

Behavioural symptoms

- Irritable
- Argumentative
- Passive/aggressive
- Increased drinking, smoking
- Compulsive actions
- Physical or verbal aggression
- Speaking in a manner that is not your usual style – fast, slow, mumbled, and so on
- Avoiding challenging situations

stomach problems (unless I have eaten something that didn't agree with me), I know I need to address the cause. You will have your own signs – headaches, shortness of breath when thinking about a particular thing, and so on. Learn to recognize those signs so you can act on them.

A word of warning here. With at least some of these symptoms, identifying them in this way might actually lead us to exacerbate them, simply because we have highlighted them as possible reasons for concern. A physical symptom such as a few heart palpitations may well be completely harmless, but it can make us feel very uneasy if we are already a little edgy. We might find our heart palpitating a little more because of our increasing anxiety over it, and rationalize it as a heart trouble when it was actually just a common palpitation. In other situations our behaviour can trigger the same behaviour in others. For example, 'I am irritable because of a particular anxiety; my partner mirrors my behaviour, which in turn fuels further my irritability.'

There is nothing like being told we might be anxious, or realizing it ourselves, to make us even more anxious. So it is important to retain a sense of balance when assessing your own symptoms, or those of others. We all have anxieties, many of them mild ones, and it would be naïve to suggest that we banish them forever. However, it helps if we listen to ourselves, and if we start to notice clusters of symptoms or a persistence of one in particular, we should take note of those signs and consider possible causes, some of which may be only too obvious. We should then look at positive, proactive solutions and coping strategies.

The physical symptoms of anxiety are the easiest to pick up on. But when it comes to subtle ones, such as self-consciousness or lack of confidence, it may take us longer to spot the signs. As a warning of the dangers of ignoring a growing feeling of anxiety, we end this exercise with Alan's story. Remember that we always look for clusters or patterns of change in ourselves that provide an indication that all is not well. A couple of nights of lost sleep should not be a cause of anxiety, and, as we said earlier, if we start to worry about it, we can simply exacerbate the situation. However, a month of broken sleep, where previously you had been a good sleeper, indicates that you need to address what might be the root cause of the problem. This is about regaining control, not about panic. Don't paralyze yourself with worry. But don't make a small problem become a bigger one by shrugging it off or ignoring it altogether.

Alan's story has a positive ending because he eventually read the signs. Make sure you don't ignore yours. But at the same time do not get into a state of paranoia about something that is relatively minor and which, with a few simple steps, you can overcome.

STUDY

CASE

Alan's story: *A case of ignoring the symptoms*

I work in local government. Not a demanding job, people might say, but it has many of the usual challenges. Constant deadlines need to be met, someone leaves but the work still has to be done, changing priorities, too many demands and too little time to fulfil them. These things are all part of the working day for me. Communications get stretched, then snap, and suddenly you realize that important meetings with colleagues and line managers get pushed lower down the order.

Of course I kept quiet, never really said anything. I didn't think about the effects the work was having on me, and the others working in the room did not say much when they heard me muttering to myself; things I'd like to say or should have said.

I took the broken sleep as normal. I thought, 'Everyone goes through this sometimes.' But my broken sleep pattern never seemed to go away. I kept my problems to myself – partners and parents have their own problems and I didn't want to trouble them. At that stage I started to get more anxious. I started to get a dry mouth and a fuzzy head, but put it down to the office humidity.

I started to find that I could not absorb things without walking away and coming back to them later. But what really concerned me was my memory. I'm not that old – late 40s – but I started to notice my forgetfulness. I remember one time walking up some stairs and, in the process, forgetting why I was doing so. I know this happens to all of us from time to time, but eventually we 'click' back in and remember. I just couldn't get my head straight enough to do so. By this stage I had made a connection between my job and my well-being. I had become very anxious about coming to work.

Eventually I went to the doctor. I had been ignoring the signs for a long time and I was relieved when he said it was work-related stress. I've been doing my job for years – the same 7.3 hours every day – and it seemed strange that I should have suddenly started to suffer the effects. But that proved to be the problem – the fact that I was doing the same thing every day.

I'm on a course now that will make me more marketable outside the organization I work for, and I've made sure that I do more socially than I did before. Internally I have got involved in a big project that gives me greater stimulation, and I have sought greater variety in my work. I can now see further ahead and this gives me a structure to work with. But I could have done so much more, so much earlier. I can remember when I was unemployed for two years. I got through that, so I'll get through this.

Exercise 2: The 'hot planets'

This exercise is particularly useful in helping us to understand better our relationships with others – an issue we explore further in later chapters. We all have 'buttons' in our heads that, when pressed, provoke certain kinds of emotive reactions in us.

EXERCISE

Opposite you will find a diagram of two heads – one filled in and one blank. Each head contains a hot 'sun', which symbolizes our ego. Circling this 'sun' are various planets – in the filled-in example there are three, namely 'work', 'religion' and 'sport'. The closer a planet comes to the sun, the hotter it gets. In other words, the closer a symbolic planet gets to our ego, the more it is likely to stir emotion in us.

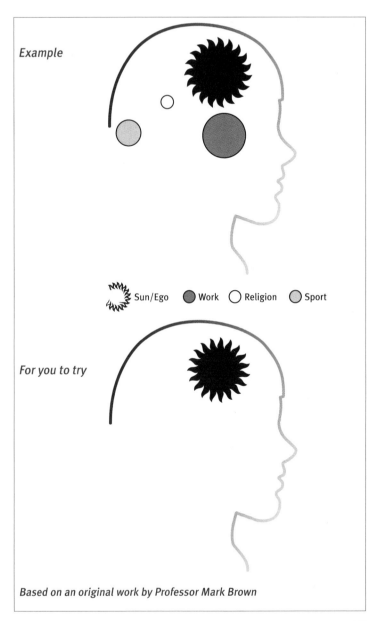

Example

For you to try

Sun/Ego ● Work ○ Religion ● Sport

Based on an original work by Professor Mark Brown

In the example we can see that 'work' is a large planet, and is located close to our sun (ego). Its proximity indicates the importance we place on our work. Its size indicates that we also have considerable knowledge and experience in our area of work.

A second planet, 'religion', is relatively small, but is still quite close to our sun. In other words we may not know much about, say, Christianity or Islam, but religion is a subject that can get us 'hot under the collar'.

The third planet, 'sport', is something about which we have a reasonable amount of knowledge, hence its medium size, but is something about which we are fairly dispassionate. We might like watching some football as a leisure activity but don't follow a particular team. It is therefore a little further from our sun than the other two planets.

Do this exercise for yourself, filling in the blank head, and adding as many or as few planets as reflects your own world. The choice of planets is entirely yours – work, religion and sport may not even be on your personal radar – but do try to be honest. There is no point in claiming expertise in one thing when actually you don't have it. Many people believe themselves, for example, to be politically knowledgeable but in fact are knowledgeable only about their own political viewpoint.

Human relationships can cause great anxiety. If we have a challenging relationship with a work colleague, for instance, the anticipation of a future meeting with that person or a demand that is made by them will make us anxious. It can help in human relationships if we understand some of our own 'hot planets' as well as those of others. Or, you could perform this exercise specifically in relation to work issues. For example, you might be the person in the diagram on page 17 one who has a large 'hot planet' called 'work' and who comes into regular contact with someone at work whose planet may be as big as yours (that is to say that they, like you, have lots of knowledge and experience in their field) but for whom work is a long way from being a central part of their life. You may well therefore find it frustrating to deal with that person, and when you have to make a demand of them at work the anticipation of doing so might make you anxious because you foresee the challenge ahead.

This brings us to another of those seven 'C's – COLLABORATION. We need to develop relationships with people with whom we may not choose to go for a drink, particularly at work, and we do this through collaboration rather than conflict. Understanding another person's world – their 'hot planets' – is an important first step towards developing a relationship with them.

In general, the planets that are furthest away from our sun (or ego) are less emotive for us, and therefore less likely to cause us anxiety.

In the chapter on relationships we will take this exercise forward as we seek to accommodate those whose 'hot planets' may be very different from our own, or indeed those whose 'planets' are very similar.

Exercise 3: Needs, wants, musts, goals

We are increasingly seeing bad fits in the early 21st century. Celebrity-obsessed cultures have led to a belief among young people, in particular, that a life as the main feature in gossip magazines is a logical career ambition, without considering the millions of alternative opportunities that are a better fit for them. Going for it because you genuinely believe you have what it takes is one thing. Trying to be someone you are not is another.

EXERCISE

You can do this exercise either alone or with a friend. Draw two crossed lines as shown in the diagram on page 20.

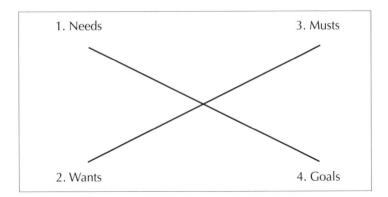

You and your friend must take an honest look at you and your life, and then each of you should write down responses to each of the four points of the cross with the help of the following questions. Ask your friend to be frank, but do not consult with him or her while you do the task.

1. What do you *need* from life?
2. What do you *want* from life?
3. What *must* you get from life?
4. What *goals* do you have in life?

When you have done this, compare your results with those of your friend and look at the differences. If you are doing this alone, think about whether the responses you gave are *really* 'you'. We often conceal our 'real self' from the world because we think others might be more impressed by the person we are trying to be. Or, because we seek peer acceptance, or even admiration, we pursue things that are a mismatch between our personality and what should be our priorities. In addition, if we see some of our character traits as weaknesses, we might decide to hide the reality from the world.

The question to ask might be: 'Do you approve of yourself? Or: 'Do you value more the approval of others?' So, did you make a career choice because *someone else* would be impressed? Do you spend lots of money in the shops because others will think highly of your capacity to spend and your buying choices?

A misalignment of your personality and priorities creates a pathway that someone else may be cutting for you. A good fit between personality and priorities means that the path is one of our own design and choosing. Look again at your list and reconsider first of all your needs. These should be simple things, which, if they were taken away, would markedly change your life for the worse. As a starting point, look around the house you live in now and ask yourself what in it fulfils a 'need' – this deals with the physical aspect. The next step is to ask what emotional and psychological needs you have – for example, what do you need from your relationships, or from your career, or from your leisure pursuits?

The problem is that we often confuse 'needs' with 'wants'. In fact, 'wants' are often superfluous to us as happy, non-anxious people, but we convince ourselves that we must have these things in order to maintain that happiness. For instance, the 'want' to be famous might be viewed, by some, as a 'need'. The pursuit of these things creates anxiety for us if they fail to fit with the kind of person we are and will become. This balance between 'wants' and 'needs' in life is an important one to strike. The aggressive pursuit of misdirected 'wants' leads to a life full of vacuums, and therefore to increased anxiety.

Similarly, we often confuse 'musts' with 'goals'. 'Musts' are things we absolutely have to do, whereas 'goals', although they have a degree of direction about them, should be fluid enough to change over time. (I am tempted to suggest that the 'musts' section could have almost nothing in it. If we are inflexible in the way we see ourselves in our world, we are likely to view things in a very limited way and to deem ourselves failures if a 'must' isn't achieved.) Goals, on the other hand, are healthy calls to action – they motivate us. But the rigid pursuit of a goal that has never changed can be paralyzing. The best goals are the ones that are defined, but where the person setting them recognizes that over time they may change.

When dealing with 'musts' we often require another of the seven 'C's – CONTROL. With a 'must' we have decided on a rigid, set course of action, but that very rigidity means that we are unable to respond to change. In essence we are controlling things we no longer need to control, because they are no longer relevant. However, if we set goals, but accept the need to change them over time, we allow ourselves to keep control over changing situations and circumstances in the way that's not possible for inflexible 'musts'.

This exercise helps us to consider our priorities honestly as we take a mental photograph of our current self. Do not be inflexible about this. We do change and our priorities change too, and our life goals will reflect these changes. However, we also see many people who do not seem able to settle down to anything and who move from job to job, house to house or even country to country. It seems that they may be searching for something outside of themselves, when the search probably needs to be done within their own mind. Being yourself and understanding who you are removes a huge anxiety as the pressure to create false identity is removed.

Exercise 4: I'm for sale! Would you buy me?

This can be a fun exercise to do and is based on an idea borrowed from Douglas Coupland's novel *Jpod*. Its power is that it can help us assess both our strengths and weaknesses, but with the intention, too, of helping us perhaps to see the funny side of those weaknesses – laughter can be a great antidote to our hang-ups. The exercise asks you simply to imagine how you would sell yourself on an internet auction site such as eBay!

EXERCISE

What would you write in your entry? You have to sell yourself, highlighting all of your best features. But you cannot tell lies, so you have to point to your faults and weaknesses too. I worked with a friend to produce the following example, which you could use as a template to do your own. Remember, have fun while you do it and bear in mind that selling anything in this way requires you to point out as many positive features as you can!

Item description:	First-born son
Current bid:	1.4 million (nowhere near reserve – this is a unique offer!)
Time left:	About 40 years if he gets on his bike a bit more
Start time:	It is never too late to start
History:	Lived a little
Location:	London, England
Ship to:	Europe, Brazil. Australia is quite nice at the moment too.
Feedback rating:	Could do better

You are bidding on a mid-1960s model Anglo-Saxon male. Considering his age, he retains youthful and occasionally puerile tastes. A good and loyal friend, and good company when in the mood, he has a strange and creative mind that dislikes conventional living and would say that his life so far has been moderately successful. As he is a supreme optimist he thinks it will become more so. Friends will be surprised to hear that, although often irritable and moody, he is happiest when in this state. Would therefore appeal to eBaying psychologists. Although prematurely greying, he retains the belief that this will reverse once his two daughters leave home.

His weaknesses are that he likes to be liked and he leaves everything to the last minute. He also considers himself to be a bit of an academic but, owing to his low boredom threshold, avoids intellectual conversation. He also has two speeds – slothful laziness and manic activity. Very good at leaving jobs half done. Or not started at all. Can get anxious when not fulfilling dreams and this can make him retire to the sofa for extended periods until he snaps out of it.

At the moment he is offering only his unique genetic code for sale. As there is only one source of this he believes that he is offering something special. Thinks that scientific advancement means that we will all come back to life one day and is therefore offering his very own genetic blueprint so that he can be in the first wave.

Secretly wants to be a long-distance lorry driver.

This is a playful exercise with a more serious side. It allows you to be honest about your vulnerabilities while, at the same time, as I suggested in the introduction to the exercise, learning to laugh at them a little. The serious element to this comes as we recognize that our vulnerabilities are often those things that make us anxious. We may view them as real weaknesses, which will then stop us acting in situations where our vulnerabilities may be tested.

Exercise 5: Signature strengths and key values

'The fact is, I no longer believe in my infallibility. That is why I am lost.'

The character Rubashov, in Arthur Koestler's *Darkness at Noon*

And now we come in for some healthy contradiction! Although I have suggested that to make an assessment of your weaknesses and vulnerabilities is important, as indeed it is, I have also said that we should not get wrapped up in self-analysis. Psychologist and writer Martin Seligman suggests we go one step further than this in his book *Authentic Happiness*. What he says is that we shouldn't spend our time trying to correct our weaknesses when that time could be better spent nurturing our strengths. This realization came to him as he was trying his best to be a good parent. He thought that maybe his time would be better spent encouraging the strengths in his children rather than fretting about their weaknesses as he saw them. This is a dilemma that many parents will recognize.

Seligman went further, and this is where you and I come in. He identified 24 'signature strengths' or moral traits (as opposed to talents, like running the 100 metres quickly). These 'signature strengths' were then incorporated across six key values – wisdom, courage, humanity, justice, temperance and spirituality.

In the table below I have taken these six key values and provided my own definition of them. The exercise is not about you assessing 'signature strengths' – readers who wish to do this can take Seligman's test on his website at www. authentichappiness.org – it's about you reflecting upon when you have demonstrated the best values that you can show to the world as a human being. Try to come up with examples of when your thoughts and actions, and your behaviour in your relationships with others, have shown you to be an upholder of those values. It is tempting to say, 'I am not worthy' or 'I have never done any of these things'. But in reality we all have shown ourselves in our best light in at least some of these values, and have shown to the world that we are capable of presenting the highest values of humankind through our thoughts and actions.

Value	Value description	When I did this
Wisdom	The knowledge and wisdom that helps us make sensible judgements and good decisions.	
Courage	Facing challenges and adversity without being diverted from the course of action we believe to be right.	
Humanity	Where we demonstrate the qualities we consider to show the best of us as human beings in our relationships with others.	

Value	Value description	When I did this
Justice	Where we treat everyone in a fair and equitable manner.	
Temperance	Where we show self-restraint. I do not suggest that this means total abstinence from pleasure.	
Spirituality	A connection with the mind and its improvement rather than material things.	

A warning about the five exercises

Knowing oneself is important. Analyzing oneself into a state of inertia is dangerous. In the world of sport there are many sportspeople who have stifled their athletic ability by over-scrutinizing the technical aspects of their game. In rare cases they have stopped being able to perform altogether. Many of us 'selectively see' certain character faults in ourselves, which we allow to become all-pervasive. If we believe ourselves to be a certain way, we look for all the behaviours that prove that belief. When we look at ourselves, a healthy appraisal of our strengths, weaknesses and character traits is beneficial. But be aware that many of us are over-critical, believing that certain character traits we identify in ourselves are fatal flaws that we will never overcome. It is known, for example, that a number of men, myself included, spend a lot of energy trying not to be like their father, and find it annoying when they display behaviour that to them mirrors that of their father. What many people do is over-analyze one aspect of their behaviour because it is in the forefront of their mind, while ignoring all the other behaviours and character traits that prove that they are a unique individual.

In fact, unless these 'flaws' lead us into immoral or illegal actions, there is little value in obsessing over them. A healthy analysis of ourselves helps us to recognize when our emotional responses are coming into play and to adapt our behaviour accordingly – as Chris Carling's quote at the beginning of the chapter suggests. She recommends a three-step approach to helping us do this:

- Practise being alert to those emotional responses that surface momentarily. Catch them before they go back underground and exert their influence without our awareness.
- Adopt a posture of curiosity and interest in what has happened. For example, 'What was that stab of irritation about when X said Y?'; 'I felt anger welling up in me just then. What was going on?'
- Name the feelings you have observed – fear, anger, excitement, annoyance and so on. Tell yourself very explicitly what you have observed. Accept it as part of you. By naming and acknowledging your feelings you'll find they exert less force and allow you greater choice in how you behave.

A happy ending...

We finish Part One with Heather's story. Heather encapsulates many of the things we have explored in this chapter – wrong assumptions about the kind of person she was and what she was suited to, combined with a lack of confidence born out of bad experiences. But, for her, what followed was a rethink, some false starts and, ultimately, a direction that allowed her to rebuild her confidence.

STUDY

CASE

Heather's story: *Being 'self-aware'*

I think my story is really about me becoming more aware of my strengths and weaknesses and also what causes stress and anxiety in me.

Prior to the job I do now, I worked as a call centre team leader for a retail service company with very high-profile clients. I had made the move into this job without being entirely sure of the direction I wanted to go in, but I did think that this might suit me. In hindsight it was entirely wrong for me, but I imagined for quite a while that it was right.

The atmosphere was fast-paced and highly pressurized. Our customers were very demanding and sometimes very rude too. Call centres are not always the most attractive places to work in, so we were often short-staffed, and this meant that we constantly had more work than we could handle. My boss didn't help. She was always up for a challenge (and was very good at creating crises herself) and seemed to thrive only when she could put her disaster recovery plan into operation. She would highlight continually the weaknesses in my team, despite the fact that I had no other assistants as other teams did, and I guess I began to think that I had real personal shortcomings. I lost confidence in myself.

This loss of confidence meant that I stopped believing that there were things that I could do to make the situation more tolerable – it was never going to perfect! I should have challenged my boss harder to try to get additional resources or to spread the workload. I should have left my work problems at work when I went home in the evening. Instead I simply worried all the time and cried a lot – even at work. My sleep pattern was terrible and I started to isolate myself. I took a holiday and didn't sleep for the entire week, getting anxious about going back there when the holiday finished. I knew then that I had to leave, which I did, even though I didn't have another job to go to.

Initially I felt better for having done this, although I was naturally concerned about starting another job. I was still suffering from a loss of confidence. I started seeing someone I had met at a party – I couldn't believe he would be interested in someone like me – but placed way too much emphasis on it, and was devastated when it ended after only a short amount of time. I was spiralling downwards quickly and had a spell on Prozac (awful nightmares) and some counselling (which helped).

But my story, I am pleased to say, has a happy ending. I realized that I needed to get some confidence back. So I took a job that was below my capability level – the fact I knew this was a sign that, deep *down, I was a capable person. Because I was good at it, it allowed me to have some success, and my confidence built up again as a result. I learnt that sometimes taking a step back, to use a cliché, can get you moving forward again. I have started to look at myself with a more balanced view. Self-help books have been of value to me. I have learned that I have always needed other people's opinions to validate my own. I have never before really done things on my own initiative because I didn't have the confidence to do so. My confidence is starting to build. I've just been promoted, so something must have worked!*

What the healthy analysis really can do is to allow us to focus on our unique talents and signature strengths and use these to generate a less anxious, happier life that suits the person we are. Many of us remain unconvinced that we have these talents, strengths and capabilities.

In Part Two of this chapter we look at the capacity we have to be confident, contributing individuals, with reduced anxiety about our place in the world.

Part Two – The confidence account

'It's a great thing when you find that you still have the ability to surprise yourself. It makes you wonder what else you can do.'

Kevin Spacey's character, Lester Burnham, in the great Sam Mendes film *American Beauty*

In this part of the chapter, we take two topics – the fear of failure (or desire for success), and the need we have as humans to be curious and therefore to learn. These two consistent elements in our lives are part of what makes us who we are, and differentiate us from almost all species – certainly in the case of failure and success. We cover them together because they both impact substantially as critical elements in one of the seven 'C's – CONFIDENCE. Success breeds confidence, but we often fail to notice our successes. Failure is merely one step on the way to mastery. We are curious animals, with an almost endless thirst for knowledge. The journey to the acquiring of knowledge can be tough, and tough situations can breed loss of confidence.

While these two elements are key to our vitality as human beings, they are also huge causes of anxiety. We ask if we are succeeding or failing regularly, and become anxious if we see ourselves as failures. If we see our lives drifting, it may be because we are not doing much to prevent the drift. Our curiosity is not driving us to try new things. Presumed failure can breed lack of confidence and, as we saw in Heather's not untypical story, the results can be unpleasant.

(i) Failure versus success

> *'If we are anguished by failure it is because success offers the only reliable incentive for the world to grant us its goodness.'*

Alain de Botton, *Status Anxiety*

De Botton's quote is not a very motivating one and I use it because we can and should challenge it. We can spend a lifetime being anxious if we allow the world to judge whether we have been successful or not. If we dance constantly to the tune of other people, or to that of the world in general, rather than to our own, we quickly lose control of our own natural rhythm. A lifetime of this means a lifetime of anxiety born out of playing continual catch-up. This is because, when we enter our teenage years, we begin to experience some of the stigmas attached to perceived failure.

We now consider success and failure and how they affect our confidence.

When failure is turned into success

Lack of confidence is a primary cause of anxiety. At worst, we believe that we have an inability to deal with life itself, so we withdraw and create those very circumstances we imagined ourselves unable to deal with. Or we believe that there are certain elements within our lives (work, money, certain other people, and so on) that we lack the confidence to cope with.

As an exercise take a piece of paper and draw a line down the middle of a blank page. At the top of the left-hand side write 'Successes' and on the right-hand side 'Failures'. Then take a look back over your adult life, since the age of 18. In the success column write down as many successes as you can possibly think of. In the failure column write down as many of your perceived failures as you can think of. Your challenge is to come up with more successes than you can failures.

A struggle? All of us have more successes than failures but many readers may well have a longer 'failure' than 'success' list. This may be due to two things:

• Not recognizing your many successes.
• Over-emphasizing perceived failure when it was the first step on the route to a success.

If you say to yourself that you failed because you are a failure, 'useless' or because you have an inherent genetic inferiority that made it impossible for you to do something, then it is likely that you have built in the ready-made responses that will make it very difficult for you ever to succeed in that particular thing.

This is usually a confidence issue. Those who lack confidence can self-perpetuate it by believing in what we call 'learned helplessness' – that is everything bad that happens to us is due to our own lack of ability. Those who succeed at certain things will have also failed along the way, but will have looked at the circumstances around which they failed and resolved to make improvements next time. Failing at something does not make you a failure. In fact none of us is a failure, but we frequently behave as though we are when we fail at something.

The reality is that many of us are able to turn failure into success and do so. Indeed, when you look at your list of successes, you may find that some of those successes appear in the failure list too. If you lack confidence in your own capabilities, think very hard about your list of successes. Single mothers, the unemployed and the person doing the job that doesn't 'fit' them are groups prone to breakdowns in confidence at a time when they need it most. In fact, think about the person who does a job they can't stand for years. That sounds like a success to me – even though I might also suggest they think about moving on!

Say, for example, you have a degree of social anxiety where you feel uncomfortable walking into a room of strangers. Your fear may have been based on previous bad experiences. But it is likely, too, that there will have been times when you have walked into a room of strangers and, though apprehensive, enjoyed yourself. We remember the bad times even though they may have been few in number.

An obvious example of where we are prepared to take 'failure' and bounce back in our quest for success is when we learn to drive. Many of us fail our test at least once, and, when I work with groups and we discuss this, we can all laugh as we share the horror stories associated with it. The critical factor is that, presuming we did pass in the end, the process, however painful, involved analyzing why we failed and putting it right until we passed. That mindset will serve us well in other situations too. What we are doing is taking CONTROL (see the seven 'C's) of the circumstances around our failure so that we may succeed next time.

When we feel we are making a contribution

Many of us lack confidence because we don't feel we make a CONTRIBUTION (see the seven 'C's). Where we do feel we make a contribution, we are more inclined to see ourselves as successful and we therefore become more confident. We value both ourselves and what we do in life. I believe that anyone who makes a contribution to the improvement of someone else's life is a success. That is not pop-psychology waffle, but to me a simple truth.

We imagine the word 'contribution' to be connected with some sort of psychological lifelong triathlon – a series of hyper-demanding challenges and achievements at the end of which someone else will assess whether we made a 'contribution' or not. That does not mean that we shouldn't be stretching ourselves. But the fact that so many of us feel that we are not really playing a part, at work for example, creates a softer, more existential anxiety, but nonetheless one that never seems to go away. You do not need to get anxious about this, or about the effect that your contributions can have, and I use a famous story to illustrate.

It concerns a beach where, every day, hundreds of starfish were washed up by the waves on to the shore to await the inevitability of death. Every day a jogger would take his morning run along the shore, and see a young man throwing some of the starfish back into the water. Every day he thought about the futility of the exercise until one day he decided to confront the young man. 'Young man,' he said, 'There are millions of starfish. You cannot hope to save them all. You cannot hope to make a difference.' At this point the young man turned, picked up a starfish, and threw it back into the water. 'Made a difference to that one,' he said.

So my advice to anyone, no matter what job they do or what role they fulfil, would be to value what you do – don't dismiss it. It may not be what you really want to do, but right now someone, somewhere, is valuing the fact that you do it. You are making a contribution but maybe you haven't realize it yet. You *are* a success.

When we feel at ease with our status

We believe that success comes from the status that society grants us. In an era when those with a talent for publicity can outshine those with other, more beneficial talents, we are under huge amounts of pressure to acquire status through fame or superficial 'achievements'. What is remarkable is that, in an era when we've never had so many opportunities or directions into which we can channel our talents, so many of us, particularly our young, are choosing to define success in an ever-narrowing bandwidth. If we need to sow the seeds of our status in society through the needle's eye of fame, then many of our younger generation will end up feeling very disappointed. Of course, it will not be quite as dramatic as this. Out of our perceived status, in part, we build our self-esteem, but the barrier to achieving status becomes clear if we allow status to be defined by someone else or by our culture.

Below a superficial level, for example, working in what might be perceived as a low-status job, we are judged more, and of course far more meaningfully, by our personality traits and by our empathy with others than by the work we do. We immediately attach higher status to the job of car mechanic if the mechanic is knowledgeable, helpful and concerned for us, than if they conform to the stereotype (no matter how wrong this is) of someone who tells you your car needs £500-worth of repairs when you only went in to have the battery changed. It applies in other professions too. When a friend of mine went to his local solicitor in a provincial French town for advice, and the solicitor asked to be paid in cash so as to avoid tax, he accorded a lower status to the job of solicitor in France for a time because of the actions of one person – even though most French solicitors will be professional and good at their job. We behave according to the status we subscribe to, no matter what we do. And according to the status we apply to others and what they do too.

So our status is, to a significant degree, self-applying; if a woman believes that her role in the home is an important one, one worthy of status, then she will act according to that perception. Her level of self-esteem will be high because she attaches high status to that role. If, however, she thinks that being a housewife is somewhat akin to the Edwardian idea of being 'in service', then her status, and her self-esteem, will be low.

I admit that applying status according to just one aspect of our lives – work – may be out of date. We live such diverse lives now that our self-esteem may rise when we fit all the different parts together. For example, we do something in our day job that we do not feel gives us status, but only because it allows us to pay for our parachuting hobby where we are the president of the local club and where we therefore have status. It may take longer for some to realize that there are many vehicles with which we can build up our self-esteem than they may have believed.

(ii) Curiosity versus 'the struggle'

Suppressing curiosity – curiosity being a natural and healthy human instinct – is far more damaging to our long-term well-being than the anxieties we may feel as we try to satisfy our curiosity. Those anxieties can be natural and healthy parts of us if we channel them productively. The point is to see anxiety as a means by which we focus our thinking and make a realistic appraisal of the way forward.

Here is a classic process we go through as we satisfy our curiosity:

1. Being curious leads us to seek out opportunities and express a desire to learn.
2. As we seek to discover, we find out many new things both about ourselves, about other people and about the world we live in.
3. Those discoveries can generate conflicting emotions. If we enjoyed doing something (with hindsight), then we feel comfortable about doing it again. If we had considerable struggles – perhaps we started our own business but were successful – then we might say that the struggle was worth it. If we didn't get to where we hoped we can either give up or resolve to do better next time. In this case we…
4. … repeat the experience – having learned from our mistakes – until we get it right.
5. Even when we are learning something new, we eventually master the process, such as learning to drive. If we are running a business, we may turn that business into a success. If our curiosity was fuelled by foreign travel, we may feel that we have a better understanding of other people's worlds and cultures.

If you have undertaken a change of direction recently, you may find it useful to map out your progress through these five phases. In phases 3 and 4, in particular, you might have found that the process was disconcerting, as you became apprehensive about the situation you were in, or unclear about the direction in which you were heading. Part of the approach to working with anxiety is to understand that our anxious feelings are entirely natural. Even those who have come to love the new direction they took will say that along the way the difficulties sometimes made them question their original choice. Recognizing that the anxiety is normal can sharpen our thoughts and refocus our thinking in the direction we have chosen. And of course this can be true even if the direction was not one that we sought ourselves.

Freud identified what he called 'the struggle', describing this period as, on reflection, the most beautiful in our lives. But the struggle can be disconcerting. When we try to find something through our curiosity we risk getting lost – particularly when we are learning, when we are discovering ourselves and when we are exploring our intellectual and emotional intelligence. Indeed, it is rare that any of us keeps to a well-trodden, easily found path as we go through life, and life would perhaps be rather unexciting if we did.

So how do we deal with the struggle? And how do we accept it as a natural part of living – perhaps as something that can be fun, and something, on reflection, we're happy to go through? Being frustrated as we 'struggle' creates anxiety: 'Am I ever going to make it?' 'Everyone else seems to be doing really well and I am not.' 'Am I the only person who feels like this?' These are typical questions we might ask ourselves.

Life at its best can, and should, be one long learning process. This has the positive effect of a richer and more productive life as we develop our curiosity, explore opportunities and increase our knowledge. As Freud suggests, however, this richness will come hand in hand with the struggle, and it may only be hindsight that tells us it was worth it. But what would you do without the struggle? Imagine you're at the end of your life – what would you like to be able to say about it? That you didn't try anything? Probably not. But by trying new things we must accept that there will be anxieties along the way. Try to value them as part of the learning experience.

Do remember that learning comes in many forms. It may be that we didn't enjoy other cultures, or that our business failed, or that the new job wasn't right for us. That's OK. We have still had a learning experience. Learning what we are not can be just as powerful as learning what we are. We now know more about ourselves – either way. If we are curious we begin to seek out the answers to questions that we weren't even consciously aware of asking, but which provide the fuel to discovery.

So where can curiosity take us? The existential anxiety we will cover in the next chapter can come into play if we suppress the curious side of ourselves. Allowing our curiosity to flourish can provide a more fulfilling life for us and give it particular meaning. Remember:

'Your brain enjoys energetic enquiry. And dies with passive acceptance.'

Source unknown

THE MEANING OF LIFE:

*'As humans we are inclined to feel that life must have a point.
We have plans and aspirations and desires. We want to take
advantage of all the intoxicating existence we've been endowed
with. But what's life to a lichen? Yet its impulse to exist, to be,
is every bit as strong as ours, arguably even stronger. If I were
told I had to spend decades being a furry growth on a rock in the
woods, I believe I would lose the will to go on. Lichens don't.
Like virtually all living things, they will suffer any hardship,
endure any insult, for a moment's additional existence. Life, in
short, just wants to be. But – and here's an interesting point – for
the most part it doesn't want to be much.'*

Bill Bryson, *A Short History of Nearly Everything*

Experts on the subject of children and learning believe that, when
young, we start asking the existential questions about life at a younger
age than was previously supposed – dispelling the notion of the
great child psychologist Jean Piaget that children started to ask these
questions from around the age of 11. When, for example, did you
start to consider the 'What do you want to be when you grow up?'
question? My six-year-old daughter is convinced that she will be
living in Spain – not that she has ever been there! Later on in life the
question may have changed, so we might ask ourselves, 'How do
I want to be remembered?' Nonetheless, the fact that we ask these

questions implies that we recognize there is a higher meaning and purpose to our lives beyond mere survival.

Living your life in a partial vacuum

In physics we use the phrase 'free space' to denote what we call the 'perfect vacuum'. That is, a space with absolutely nothing in it. In reality, in both physics and real life, the perfect vacuum does not exist. Instead, we have things called 'partial vacuums', with some 'stuff' going on, even if it is very little. Partial vacuums in our life are boring, and yet it is one of the paradoxes of the human experience that when we do get a bit of time on our hands to do some of the things we'd like to do, we often do nothing – or at least nothing that is meaningful! Look, for example, at what happens to some people when they retire – at a time when there is never a greater need to keep active, a significant number of people do the opposite. Think about what we do when we get home after a hard day at work: could we sacrifice an evening in front of the TV to do something more meaningful? We know we probably should but often we don't.

It is worth remembering that we are all born into partial vacuums. Each of us has a choice about the extent to which we fill that vacuum. If we fill it to capacity, then we substantially increase the internal pressure. We can all tolerate different amounts of pressure. The more the pressure is personally rewarding, and the more suited to utilize our particular strengths and talents it is (see Martin Seligman's 'signature strengths' in the last chapter), then the more pressure we can take.

Filling the vacuum – lessons from history

Just as Sweden produced a generation of great tennis players in the 1980s, and the USA a line of great jazz musicians in the 1940s and 1950s, Austria spawned three of the most important figures in the whole history of psychiatric study: Sigmund Freud (born 1856), his student Alfred Adler (1870), and, a little later, Viktor Frankl (1905).

These three created a body of work that is critical for the student of anxiety and the neuroses connected with it, and provides immense food for thought for the person trying to understand their own behaviours and motivations, as well as those of others. In addition, they asked the bigger question of why we are actually here.

Of course, when we look at what they said, and in particular Viktor Frankl, it helps to remember that there is no ultimate wisdom about this question or about the answers – although some of us at least search hard to try to find some sort of purpose or meaning. It may be that one day the study of ourselves becomes an exact science (I personally hope that never happens) but, until that day, we have to rely on the best-informed estimates of those who spent a lifetime studying 'us' to help 'us'. These three giants of psychiatry differed greatly in the way they believed we 'tick' – although they shared more than they would care to admit if they were alive now.

Sigmund Freud believed that a critical driver in our behaviour is the accessing of certain kinds of pleasure and, in particular, the need for sexual pleasure. But other pleasures, such as food and the accessing of leisure time, could also be included in what he called the 'will to pleasure'. One can immediately relate this to the anxieties we see in early 21st century society regarding sexual potency, sexual drive, sexual competitiveness, and so on. Why is it, for example, that such huge swathes of the media devote themselves to making us believe that everyone has more sex than we do? (And I differentiate between sex and sex with someone you love.) And why is it that our current obsession with matters sexual, and the anxiety we get from these, is so prevalent in modern society? It would seem that the media are well aware of the primeval connection they make between selling magazines and newspapers, and our desire for more sex ourselves.

I must confess to reading the *National Enquirer* (for entertainment value!) and considering the possibility that some of it might be true. As I read it I wonder how, with all the sex they appear to be having, any of the people featured in it have any time for singing, acting or whatever it is they do professionally. I'm sure that, if he were alive today, Freud would argue that the current fashion for body piercing in erogenous areas merely backs up what he said all along, or that the massive increase in the availability of pornography in the late 20th century reflects this 'will to pleasure' perfectly. What is clear is that Freud made a compelling connection between sex and angst, even if critics say that the connection was overstated. Ask yourself how many times you can recall thinking about sex today.*

Alfred Adler saw the driver in us as the 'will to power'. In his opinion, this is what enables us to demonstrate superiority and, conversely, the anxieties and neuroses we potentially develop when we perceive our own inferiority and weakness – what he referred to as the 'inferiority complex'. Corporate motivators will be pleased to read that he propounded our desire to achieve goals through self-actualization as a method to achieving this superiority. He recognized that our goals do change over time, and that this wasn't necessarily about some kind of life mission, but that our perceived failure to achieve these goals causes the sense of inferiority that creates, among other things, anxiety about our capabilities. Those who have an inferiority complex begin to self-reflect, and, while this is valuable, it can also be damaging if the degree to which we self-reflect becomes overwhelming or the reactions to it adverse.

We finally come to Viktor Frankl, who, being in the next wave of thinkers, had the advantage of being able to look back at the work of Freud, Adler and others. Frankl argues that the primary driver in human behaviour was the search for meaning in our lives. He referred to what he called the 'existential vacuum' – that is, the gap we have in our lives when we feel that life has little or no meaning, which arrives because the freedom of the healthy human spirit has in some way become restricted or blocked. Where this restrictiveness occurs (the 'vacuum' he refers to), we start the process of 'filling the vacuum' (because we are intelligent enough to do so), then engineer into the

---

* I do not want to be seen as the next in a long line of writers who wants to trivialize Freud by concentrating only on sex. He clearly had much to say that was groundbreaking, particularly in relation to his work on the unconscious mind, even if his work polarizes people. I merely use his work on sex to illustrate the point about primary causes of anxiety in 21st century society and what their sources might be.

gaps a series of things that our imagination tells us will give us some further purpose to living other than 'being'. In many ways it is an admirable quality that we feel the need to fill the gaps. We realize soon enough that we are not immortal (and what an 'anxiety-ridden' moment that was) and many of us begin to recognize the need to create purpose for ourselves.

Frankl's writings reflect his supreme confidence in the triumph of the human spirit – the spirit he refers to means all of the internalized resources and capabilities we have to live with dignity and meaning, in whatever situation we find ourselves. When the spirit becomes blocked, then the full value of that spirit, and its remarkable power, also become blocked and we either struggle to create meaning or we fill the gaps with things that create superficial meaning. Perhaps the filling up is done with some of the things that Adler and Freud talked about – the pursuits of pleasure and power – as well as other things.

We have seen some of the reasons why the giants of psychological study believe that we try to fill the partial vacuums we experience with power, gratuitous pleasure or invented necessities in order to add meaning to our lives. One day we might get to know who was right and who was wrong, but I suspect that the answer is that they were probably all right.

Most of us have experienced 'partial vacuum' phases, during which the ways we have tried to fill the gap may have diminished us as human beings. So how might we go about filling it in a more useful way? How might we give meaning to our lives, and by so doing reduce anxiety in even the toughest and most horrifying of situations?

It is difficult to compare ourselves to lichens (referring back to the Bryson quote at the beginning of the chapter), and for many of us it is not a particularly exciting prospect just to 'be'. But, nonetheless, those 'plans, aspirations and desires' to which he refers seem to be creating the need for a degree of complexity in our lives that can cause a great deal of anxiety. Many of us are in a hurry, which is curious since we now live longer than any of our predecessors did. The urgency to 'fill the gap' in north European societies possibly comes about because of the decline of organized religion, and the desire to obtain more out of life than mere survival.

Believers in an afterlife *may* (and I say that reservedly) see life on earth as only a part of a never-ending continuum, where the pressure to achieve is tempered by the belief that there is much more to come afterwards. Europe may have become the secular centre of the world, with many, while not saying outright that they don't believe, demonstrating an indifference to organized or disorganized religion. There is evidence to suggest that the rise in religious indifference has a parallel with increased wealth in societies. In the USA, the recent increase in Christian belief is strongest in the middle part of the country. The two coastlines – the wealth generators of the American economy – are very different from what we know as 'Middle America'. So does that imply that once we have wealth, we are confronted with the paradox that, beyond a certain level, wealth is not filling the gap we thought it would, and we need something else? That we have plenty to live with, but increasingly little to live for (or so we believe)? This gap creates the classic existential anxiety so prevalent in modern society.

Ten ways to create real meaning and reduce anxiety

'A meaningful life is one that joins with something larger than we are – and the larger that something is, the more meaning our life has.'

Martin Seligman, *Authentic Happiness*

The main aim of this chapter is to look at ways in which we can try to attach meaning to our own lives and thereby reduce a particular kind of anxiety. There are many techniques and modes of thinking among 'the ten ways to create meaning' that would fit equally well in a number of the other chapters. However, the need for meaning in our lives is so fundamental to the study of anxiety that I have devoted a chapter of the book to it for that very reason. As you read other chapters, you may find it useful to cross-reference back to this one.

Do also bear in mind that not all of the ten ways will apply to you all of the time and will not always be easy to implement. For example, (vii) 'Look for meaning in apparent personal tragedy' will clearly apply, thank goodness, only in particular circumstances, and will require a personal search that is deeper than we may have experienced in our lives up to that point. Others, such as the need for humour and laughter, are easier to access if we want choose a frame of mind that will let laughter and humour in.

(i) Access your spiritual self

As a person who doesn't follow a religion this is perhaps the toughest one for me, as the author, to cover! I go here first out of my admiration for those who have found ways to transcend what I would consider to 'create meaning' in my own life, by having a place to go to that does it for them instantly. I imagine, however, that those same people would agree that spirituality was not the *only* thing to create meaning in their lives, and that the other nine ways that follow would also apply.

If you see this world as a preparation for the next, then one must assume that you have all the motivation and meaning you need in order to make this existence a fulfilling one for you. However, spirituality goes beyond questions about the accessibility of the afterlife and the preparation for it. There are of course many religions in addition to the mainstream ones of Christianity, Islam, Judaism, Hinduism and Buddhism, and many people who refer to themselves as 'spiritual' though not 'religious'. It is interesting that the UK has among the lowest number *per capita* of people in the world who describe themselves as 'religious' but the second highest (after India) who see themselves as 'spiritual'. And many in the UK and elsewhere describe themselves as 'humanists' (even if they are not certain what that means), seeing themselves as living life according to a code of morals, ethics and principles unconnected to religious belief, although these may well be shared with those who do have religious belief.

I would contend that those who don't like the idea of exploring their spirituality – perhaps it feels too 'soft' – don't have to. It is really just about connecting with things other than obvious material possessions, and digging deeper into an inner world of emotion, feeling, empathy and concern for others.

Allow the next nine ways to create meaning to enter your thinking and behaviour and the issue of 'spirituality' becomes academic. You will be 'spiritual' if you want to see yourself as such, and all of the experiences you have in life can provide nourishment if you wish it that way.

To conclude, then, historically those who have had a faith have had all the meaning they could ever need available through the teachings of their religious figureheads, but with more of us now choosing to move away from religion, that meaning still needs to be found. For those who don't have this religious connection, spiritual meaning can come in many other ways. The spiritual values that religions espouse are often the values that relate to being a good human being, and are not confined to religious belief.

What you can do

We are good at nourishing ourselves materially. But can you find ways to nourish yourself spiritually? Having a god works for some. But if you cannot believe in a god, try to search inside yourself for emotional qualities that will allow you to have a more rounded, less selfish view of yourself, the world and the people in it.

Try to look beyond the superficial into a world with a deeper, more meaningful and perhaps more altruistic engagement. Empathy is a particularly powerful emotional driver here.

(ii) Be part of the universe, but not the whole of it!

Happiness means forgetting yourself.

Self-absorption – the perspective that everything in the world is defined by our own ego – is a primary source of anxiety. It is a sign that we have recognized the need to fill the partial vacuum but that we have chosen to fill it by placing too much emphasis on self-reflection. In the preceding chapter we looked at the need to understand ourselves – what makes us unique, what our real likes and dislikes are, and so on – but it is possible to go beyond this into an indulgent absorption. We have all spent time with people who want to talk about themselves continuously – this is often a sign of their lack of confidence and an uncertainty about their place in the world.

Many of our anxieties are created through suggestion. If I pick up the newspapers this morning I can be anxious about war in the Middle East, the price of oil, or the nature of my government. But I can also be anxious about the 'fight against flab', sexual dysfunction, whether I am wearing the right clothes on the beach this summer, or about a quarter of a per cent rise in interest rates. When others suggest things about which we should be anxious, we immediately transpose those anxieties on to our own circumstances: 'Can I pinch an inch?', 'Will I be able to maintain an erection/reach orgasm?' (I get about 20 junk emails on this every day), or 'Does my swimming costume look "last year"?'

Those who worry about these things, where that worry is totally unnecessary, are probably doing so because they have little in their lives that is giving them real meaning. These are the concerns of rich, post-industrial economies, where life is comparatively easy and where our need for a degree of anxiety – which is a necessity for most of us – is translated into fears about our personal adequacy when compared with others. We can be made to believe almost anything if we are told it enough times.

In one of his writings, Frankl talks of a woman who had been sexually abused when she was young, and how in her adulthood she had gone on to have a fulfilling, satisfying sex life. However, when it was suggested to her that she should expect to have problems given her past, and that, under the circumstances, for her to be the way she was sexually was unusual, she began to have difficulties experiencing the satisfaction she had had no problem with before.

Ask whether your anxieties are a result of too much thinking about yourself, and if this is being done because of the lack of meaning and fulfilment in your current existence? And ask yourself, if friends really do judge you on your sex life, the kind of car you drive or the clothes you wear, whether these are friends you really need at all. We can be made to worry about almost anything if we want to. But we can choose not to.

What you can do

If you believe that self-absorption has made you anxious, you may find it useful to engage in activities that take you away from an over-emphasis on self-reflection. In the same way that new parenthood immediately takes one's thoughts away from superficial, self-created anxieties, there are many things you can do to draw your attention away from yourself. For example, could you give two hours of your time a week to a voluntary activity? Could you get involved in community programmes?

This is an exercise in learning to park your ego. You combine benefit to society (and deeper spiritual nourishment) with a more balanced reflection on your own anxieties.

(iii) Accept that you are not immortal

One of the great anxieties, and one that we choose to hide from in western societies, is the fact that the one certainty in life is death. As we get older we recognize that we are not the immortal person we believed we were in our teens and 20s. We start to search for things that might define us, while at the same time hoping that, when our turn comes, we do not know about it. This certainty is a major source of anxiety in us – an anxiety that some of us never shake off, and which, paradoxically, may take us nearer to death itself if the anxiety becomes too overwhelming.

There are some things we can do to alleviate this anxiety. If you, like me, see this as a real fear, then seek to overcome your thoughts about mortality by considering some or all of the following ways of looking at the world.

Your contribution will always be valuable

In a previous book on spotting and taking opportunities in life, I said that, at the end of our lives, many of us would want to look back and say that we 'had a go'. What kind of 'go' we had will differ for each of us. Ultimately, not all of us will reach the stratospheric heights that the misguided define as the only badge of success. Your contribution, however, will come in many forms and will be valuable.

We are likely to be valued by the CONTRIBUTION (see the seven 'C's) we made, and by how much we were prepared to give to improve the quality of life for others. When we read autobiographies of those in the limelight, it is interesting that many of them – particularly those who have been around for longer – like to emphasize the contributions they have made beyond their vocation. High-profile personalities such as Bill Gates, Bono and Bob Geldof are keen to go beyond the superficiality of what they do for a living, into living for what they really now want to do. The first two are still somewhere near the peak of success in their original vocation, but they, too, recognize the need to make what they would see as a worthwhile contribution while continuing to pursue that vocation.

Even more admirable are those millions upon millions of people (like you, perhaps?) who make a contribution in many unpublicized walks of life and who are sustained by doing so. The midwife, the nurse and the charity worker, for example. And, yes, the ethical financial advisor, the person who sells you a second-hand car that works, and the train driver who gets hundreds of us to work on time.

If you don't feel that you make a contribution through your job, and you feel the need to do so, change your job or look for an activity outside work that does this for you. For some of us, at least, the sense of contribution will come from the creative legacy we leave behind, or from the knowledge that we made the world better for someone else. For example, the book we wrote, the thing we invented, the scientific breakthrough or the political achievement. But also the bypass we protested against, the voluntary work we did or the donations we made to charity.

Look to future generations

Knowing that our genetic material will pass on to our children and grandchildren helps us to believe that we do carry on. Even if it is not in the tangible, conscious form we would like, many of the older generation report that this gives them one of their greatest pleasures. So be good to your grandparents and parents – family squabbles are pointless!

One day, science might bring us back!

If you want to believe that there is another life, but you have no religious belief, there is always science to turn to. Imagine that we attributed a value of 100 to the sum of all possible scientific knowledge: it is likely that the sum of our current knowledge is less than 1. We know little about time dimensions, genetic recreation or the billions of stars and planets out there. We know less about what exists at the bottom of the sea than about what is on the moon.

There is clearly a huge amount we have yet to discover, but perhaps our increasing knowledge of these things will make it possible for us to come back one day. We have a long way to go to understand the true nature of our soul, brain, bladder, cells, genes, mitochondria and so on. Key people in every generation have claimed that there is little left to know in their field, only for the next generation to challenge that notion. Some people might laugh at those who believe in cryogenics, for example. But if the idea of it helps those who have a fear of death to come to terms with it, then it at least partially removes a major anxiety for them. And, of course, there is always the possibility that they could be right – have you heard about the man who has recently left all his money in his will to himself?

Find a community that satisfies your needs

With the exception of hermits, even the most solitary of people connect with others in some way. We have places where we feel particularly comfortable (cities, towns, villages, cultures and so on) as well as groups of people whose company we prefer. This sociability provides wonderful insulation against the brutalizing freedoms of what social philosopher Jean-Jacques Rousseau called 'the state of nature'. Unlike any other creature, we can all rationalize – operate with logic and reason – and this tells us with what kinds of environments we prefer to associate ourselves. This, combined with our need to socialize, creates the communities of which we are a part. But our communities do so much more than provide a base reason for our survival.

The challenge is to find the communities that resonate with you. Do you live in the area that you really want to live in? Is your social circle just 'there because it is there'? Or does it provide you with a substantial amount of emotional nourishment? What kinds of clubs, social gatherings, leisure activities stimulate you? And, of course, community can mean your extended family, too.

It is always helpful not to limit yourself only to those who are most obviously like you. Life opens up and becomes more interesting and enriching if we are willing to engage with those who are apparently very different from us, but who provide us with new and potentially stimulating perspectives.

If we are energetic and active in our communities then we may find that long-term fears and anxieties about mortality, illness, loneliness and empty space are removed from our thoughts. We are, of course, also filling that partial vacuum with contributions that benefit both ourselves and our communities, and not with superfluous wants that fail to nourish us meaningfully. When I speak of community here, the key is not to reflect only on what you take, but also on what you give. It is true to say that, in most situations, the more you are able to give, the greater the personal returns will be, although that should not be the primary motivation for doing so.

I refer you again to the Seligman quote from earlier in this chapter: 'A meaningful life is one that joins with something larger than we are – and the larger that something is, the more meaning our life has.' This need that he identifies for a connection with something bigger than we are can be seen as inspiration for those who suffer from fears and anxieties, whatever form they take.

See yourself as being a part of nature

The latest genetic research suggests that, with a couple of anomalies, we are all descended from seven families of the evolving *Homo sapiens* species, who moved out of Africa around 25,000 years ago. Seeing ourselves as part of a continuum of the most amazing living creation that our planet has yet seen, and as a conduit into the evolution of something that may be very different from what we are now, can provide each of us with all the purpose we could hope for.

What you can do

For every way in which you believe that you are 'significant', can you find ways to balance this with ways in which you are 'insignificant'? The list of significant things – parenthood, work, unique genetic code, and so on – adds value and purpose to our chosen direction. The 'insignificant' list – one of six billion people, part of a transient, fast-evolving species, incredibly short life – serves as a valuable counterweight to an over-inflated sense of your importance.

Try making your own balanced list.

(iv) Find the joy – even in adversity

It is a curious thing that the people who are best able to deal with challenges are the ones who produce the less obvious reactions to those challenges. Here are some stories to illustrate this point.

> **Story 1:** A 76-year-old man called Charles always took his dog out with him wherever he went. He would often pop round to his local shop, leaving his dog outside while he bought his newspaper. One day, Charles bought his paper and headed back home only to be confronted by his wife Margaret. 'Where is the dog?' she asked. Charles had, of course, left the dog behind. At 76 years old, he had been experiencing some memory lapses over the last few years but, understanding that this can happen in advanced age, the couple decided to laugh about it. They could have, as many do, worried themselves

over it, checked Charles into the doctor's and probably accelerated any signs of ageing through their own anxieties about the incident.

Story 2: A group of 'prisoners', the great psychotherapist Viktor Frankl among them, had just finished a hard day's work in the Auschwitz concentration camp. Malnourished, exhausted and disease-ridden, they returned to their camp with the prospect of little food and another day of hard labour. Amidst the grimness, one of the 'prisoners' was able to point out a stunning sunset in the distance and encourage fellow prisoners to come and have a look at it. (Imagine being able to access that 'joy in adversity'! Accessing that joy gives us a reason to live.)

Story 3: There once was a woman who had a potentially fatal illness. Few of her friends knew that she had this illness, so when one of her friends was told, she was shocked because she had never had an inkling. But then she thought, 'Why should I have noticed?' The fact that her friend was living her life, full of humour, full of achievement and full of ambition, told her all she needed to know about her attitude. As she reflected on her friend, she saw someone with a sharpened sense of fun and perspective – those things having come, perhaps, from the challenge she faced. This woman's bravery amazed her, and reminded her of her own frailties.

What you can do

It is important to find joy, pleasure and contentment in moments of adversity and great seriousness. Try some of the following:

- Look for some good news in bad news stories.
- Ask what it is that makes some people happy and some not.
- Look at your world as it is – not as you imagine it to be.
- Like Viktor Frankl admiring the Auschwitz sunset, look for the joy.
- Allow yourself to be consumed by captured moments of spontaneity. Simple things like having a great meal at home with friends, lots of laughter, and so on. Do you really need to be anxious about doing the washing up?

- Tell yourself that a joyless state is an anxious one. Joy relieves anxiety.
- Above all, laugh at yourself!

(v) Allow yourself the freedom of choice

The very fact that we organize ourselves as social beings means that we compromise complete freedom of choice for other benefits. Of course, in some situations our freedom is compromised beyond a degree that we find tolerable. It can be the denial of freedom at work to do the job we want to do in the way we want to do it. It can mean the imposition of laws by governments, which go beyond what is acceptable to us. Or it can be the removal of complete physical freedom. But no matter what freedoms are taken from us, there is one thing we are free to choose and that is our attitude to that situation.

The thinking here is that if those in the most serious of situations are able to confront their circumstances with dignity, then we, with our relatively minor challenges, should be able to choose an attitude that is likely to be the most productive for us in that challenge.

For the person looking to overcome anxiety, it is about personal responsibility and the option to choose a positive approach. Even those whose anxieties are deep and require a clinical approach will recognize that, although the help and guidance of others is crucial, the indivisible element is the need for us ultimately to choose our attitude in confronting the challenge. We have to decide to help ourselves in order for others to be able to help us. We can transcend ourselves, our environment and the negative instincts connected to these simply by choosing the right attitude.

So how does this link with the search for meaning? We turn again to Frankl for this quote from *Man's Search for Meaning*:

'If [suffering] is avoidable, the meaningful thing to do is remove its cause, for unnecessary suffering is masochistic rather than heroic. If, on the other hand, one cannot change a situation that causes his suffering, he can still choose his attitude.'

What you can do

Try this. We all get days when we just don't feel like it – whatever *it* is. Write down a list of positive attitudes and approaches – say, ten – that you could adopt. And then pick one of them. Try to sustain that attitude, no matter how you feel, for as long as you possibly can on that day.

People pick up on our moods very quickly and act as mirrors that reflect our attitudes back to us. Choose a good attitude and the reflection will be a positive one, which will further accentuate the positive attitude we have chosen.

(vi) Look out at the world

> *'If you judge people, you have no time to love them.'*

Mother Theresa

Using a technique I have called 'psychological travelling' in other books, the anxious person can find it helpful to take themselves out beyond the confines of their inner world and into other worlds in order to help create meaning. Those worlds can be the personal worlds of the six billion (at last count) co-inhabitants of our earth, or the worlds of other cultures and sub-cultures. Or they can be the worlds of leisure pastimes, hobbies, exercise, religion or history. In fact they can be almost anything.

The technique involves constructing positive possibilities in our minds that challenge us and, like an adventurer, for example, we get energized by the new things we see. This is about making a conscious effort to fill the partial vacuum with things that stimulate and provide new and fulfilling avenues in which we can advance and enrich our lives.

The biggest barrier to psychological travelling is to say to yourself, 'I am as I am,' or 'I know what I like,' without any acknowledgement that, over the course of a lifetime, we are very capable of adopting a more flexible open-minded approach that will allow us to see a wider panorama of possibilities when challenged.

Is it not a horrifying thought that you might have formed your world view at 18, and still see the world that way at 60 or 70? But there are plenty of people who do just that. A world view formed so young means a life of anxiety, when all life's ups and downs challenge a very fixed, rigid understanding of it. A suppleness of outlook helps to generate a suppleness of approach when it is most needed. But, more than that, it gives us a place to go to when we have to encounter the stresses of modern living. Living in all those stresses does not make us better able to overcome them. Being able to escape them increases the possibility of relaxing the mind so that it is better able to generate a variety of solutions.

External things that give us stimulation draw us away from an over-emphasis on ourselves and our feelings of inadequacy, weaknesses and lack of what we might perceive (perhaps misguidedly) as success. To the person prone to anxiety, the psychological and/or physical escape promised by this kind of 'travel' of the mind and body can act like the valve that releases the gas in an over-full pressurized container. Sometimes we need to draw our attention away from ourselves. Like the adventurer, we can begin to see the possibilities of taking ourselves to previously unseen places if we want.

What you can do

Take a situation that has caused you anxiety in the past or one that is currently causing you anxiety. Write down how you are currently seeing that situation. Then adopt the perspective of another person, someone you know or indeed someone well known whom you don't know. How might they see it? Find inspiration in the different perspective.

(vii) Look for meaning in apparent personal tragedy

'Even the helpless victim of a hopeless situation, facing a fate he cannot change, may rise above himself, may grow beyond himself, and by so doing change himself. He may turn a personal tragedy into a triumph.'

Viktor Frankl, *Man's Search For Meaning*

With the word 'tragedy' being used to cover a whole multitude of things, from someone's sporting failure to having your new car stolen, it is worth reminding ourselves what a tragedy actually is. The death of those who die 'too young', serious illness, your children passing away before you, or losing part of one's life through wrongful imprisonment, all fall within the realm of true tragedy. This is one of the toughest things for any psychologist, writer or counsellor to write about when one hasn't experienced it for oneself. We are almost beyond anxiety here. Readers who have experienced any of these things – and of course this list is not exclusive – will have felt that the future has no purpose without one of the things that made the present immediately valuable to them. And it is difficult to say to those who are currently living these tragedies to find meaning in them without sounding patronizing.

But meaning *can* be found, and we turn once again to Viktor Frankl, who expresses beautifully in his writing where he managed to find meaning for himself and where he observed it in others. Frankl's personal story has been well told, but it bears repeating: four years in Aushwitz and Dachau concentration camps, the murder of his wife, mother, father and brother, the appalling conditions in which he was made to work and the witnessing of an endless barbarity inflicted on his fellow prisoners and, of course, on himself. Frankl survived, and was able to recount his experiences in his seminal book *Man's Search For Meaning*, but his experiences also informed much of his other writings and teachings as well as his work as a psychotherapist.

Where the future apparently holds little for us, how can we hope to find any meaning in the present, or any sense that we can make an optimistic connection between our life in the present and what is to come? With absolutely no prospect of a future at all, the only recourse is to create meaning in one's circumstances through dignity and courage.

But where there is a future, or where current circumstances are so intolerable that it is difficult to see a future, we can still take ourselves to a world of spiritual richness that transcends those circumstances. That world can help us create meaning in any circumstances. For many of Frankl's fellow survivors it meant having conversations with wives and loved ones, even though they were not there. For Frankl it also meant creating things to live for. His lifeline was to recreate the manuscript for a book (which eventually became *Doctor and the Soul*), which he had had to give up when in the camp, despite having stitched it into his trouser lining. He spent time recreating his manuscript using traded writing materials and scraps of paper. He gave himself a reason – what we might call a 'Why?' – to live for.

The 'Why?' to live for doesn't apply only to extreme situations like Frankl's – we all create 'Whys?' all the time. It is just that in modern society we often create 'Whys?' that are so superficial they provide little spiritual nourishment.

What you can do

For those working through the circumstances suggested in the title of this section, the following ideas might help a little:

- **Take time:** In tough circumstances we may not be able to see any way forward, but it might be that we need a lot of time to make any necessary psychological adjustments. We should give ourselves that time and recognize that feelings of helplessness and desperation are natural and normal human reactions. Do not feel guilty for wanting 'time'.

- **Be realistic:** Things will never be the same as they were before but we can, given time, reach a position of acceptance. The current vogue word is 'closure', but that is not what this is about. The door to the past is never 'closed' and it doesn't have to be. But we can have more than one door open at the same time.

- **Take small steps:** Don't try to move at unrealistic speeds. In any tough personal challenges, try to think what could be the very smallest step you could take into the future. The first positive action we take is the smallest step imaginable. It sets us off in a good direction, even if the journey will be a slow one.

- **Remember – there are many ways to be with someone you love:** In circumstances where we have lost the very thing that gave life meaning, and real love is quite clearly one of those things, we can use the person we love as a crucial support in the future. I use a touching story to illustrate here:

An acquaintance of mine, while backpacking across Australia, came across an English woman in her mid-60s. She spent the next two weeks with her and began to learn a little more about her. Her husband had died two years earlier and she had had to rethink the remaining years of her life and what she wanted to do with them. One day she gathered her whole family together and told them that she was going to be away for four years while she travelled the world. She told them not to worry, that she would be taking it slowly, would be returning home regularly and that any of them were welcome to join her on any stage of her journey and share the experience. And she added that, although her husband had died, she would be very conscious of 'taking him with her'.

What was interesting to me was that this woman had apparently felt no need to do this travelling when her husband was still alive, but it had become a huge desire once he had gone. I took other things from her story, too, that can be useful in circumstances other than bereavement. The first was that sometimes we have to make a change in our life in order to access a way of life that can allow us to accept what has happened, but which doesn't mean we have to blank out memories. The second was that, although the pursuit of happiness in adversity requires an element of 'me' in one's thinking, the fact that this lady had invested much time in reassuring her family meant that she was fully in tune with the emotions of others. Would her trip have been half as enjoyable if she hadn't prepared the ground with concerned family members beforehand? One of the things I have noticed about those who have been through tough times is that their sense of empathy is often amplified. This is a powerful and admirable emotional characteristic.

The third thing that struck me about this story was that it reminded me of something that I know is important in my own life, and which others tell me is so in theirs. It is that, even reaching as far back as our youth, many of us have had this feeling that there is something we must do before our own time is up. Of course, in our youth we had no concept of the end, but as we start to see our life accelerating ahead, the need to do the thing that calls us becomes greater. This is a philosophical point, but many of us have an inner voice that tells us things about ourselves. This 'calling' could relate to work, hobbies, family or, in the case of our travelling widow, a curiosity about the world that needed to be satisfied and helped to carry her through bereavement.

If another example of finding a calling in adversity were needed, it would be the remarkable response of Colin Parry when his 12-year-old son Tim was murdered by the IRA in Warrington in the UK in 1993. His charity and campaigning work, combined with his dignity in suffering, are inspirational.

(viii) Remember – everything happens for a reason, if we want there to be one

We all know about the great success Winston Churchill had as a wartime leader. But many will not know about his prolonged periods of depression (what he called his 'black dog'), his political failures (India, Gallipoli), his serious illnesses (including a dangerous operation for the time), and the many years of political isolation. Churchill may have been a bulldog, but he was an anxious and emotional one. He had no qualms about crying in an era when men didn't do it and he perhaps recognized that, in his struggle, the seeds were being sown for what made his life, at the end of it, a fulfilling one. Fulfilling enough at least for him to say on his deathbed, 'I am content.'

Sigmund Freud believed that the challenges that life throws up are a necessary part of long-term contentment. We need contrasting experiences and emotions to attach meaning to our lives. When we are confronted with struggles it is important to separate those struggles into the parts we can have some control and influence over and those we can't. If we can attach meaning to 'the struggle' – recognizing that there might be a reason for it, we are better able to compartmentalize or suspend that which we can't control. We focus our energy on those parts of 'the struggle' that we can control.

The Dalai Lama suggests that we spend most of our lives exploring possibilities. But he says that those possibilities are not always going to give us happy experiences – for example, we choose the wrong job or the wrong partner. Buddhist teachings suggest that this exploration of possibilities can lead us to the point where we find our calling, and we thus begin to see meaning, if we want to, in all the struggles we have had along the way.

There is a challenge here that is so important for those who have, for example, anxieties relating to the job they do. If your job is not the right one for you, the obvious answer is to look for another one. But there clearly are ways of looking for another one and ways of analyzing your discontent with the current one. If you are in this situation, and I guess many readers are, then there are two questions to ask:

- **Is the problem my employer? Is it a bad organization to work for, for whatever reason?**
  Think carefully about this. Unless you assume that all employers are bad, what makes yours fundamentally worse than others? Or worse than an employer operating in the same field as you?
- **Is the problem my attitude to the job?**
  Again, think carefully here. Coming into any job with a negative attitude, even if there may be some justification for it, will create those very circumstances you fear. You may be blind to the good because you want to see only bad.

What you can do

We saw at the end of the last chapter the value we can place on using experiences as a way of learning. If you believe that things happen for a reason, you can assess what that reason is, and then consider what you have learnt from the experience. Writing this down may reinforce it better in your own mind than just pondering it in your head.

(ix) Tell yourself – 'I *can* get better'

The great French psychotherapist Emile Coué pioneered a technique known as 'auto-suggestive optimism', which informs much writing in the field of popular positive psychology to this day. Coué suggested that, by continually reciting positive mantras to ourselves, without reflecting too hard on the problems we have, we can get ourselves into the frame of mind where we believe that the positive thing we have said to ourselves will happen. (Or at least to the point where we increase the chances of making that thing happen.) We see it commonly in professional sport: the sprinters at the beginning of the Olympic 100m sprint final tell themselves that they are going to win, and almost hypnotize themselves into believing it.

Coué based his work on a discovery he made early in his career. When giving treatments to a group of people suffering illness, he made a series of highly positive statements to some of them about the medicine he was giving them. To others he said nothing. In assessing recovery rates, he soon began to notice that those who recovered most quickly had been told positive things about the medicine they were being administered. We hear similar stories to this even now. If you tell a group of people that a drug they are being given for illness is fantastic (even though it may be useless), a surprisingly high number will believe it and will start to overcome their illness through their own suggestive positivity.

The mantra he came up with in connection with illness was: 'Every day, in every way, I'm getting better and better.' What works for illness can also work for anxiety, and more particularly for the root causes of that anxiety, whatever it may be. When dealing with very tough personal challenges we should never underestimate the incredible capability we have to bring about the positive circumstances we envisaged.

Some say that we are really in the field of quack popular psychology here, and Martin Seligman, for one, is critical of this approach. These people could be right (and for them it is of course a self-fulfilling prophecy), but when it comes down to it, whatever label we choose to attach to it, the approach clearly works for many people with great anxiety-inducing circumstances – from bereavement and illness through to sport and workplace challenges.

What you can do

This approach has its genesis in the way we view the future and in how we learn to be optimistic about the future. Optimism, according to the great contemporary psychologist Martin Seligman, can be learned. (You might like to refer to Seligman's book *Learned Optimism: How to Change Your Mind and Your Life* for more on this.)

He suggests a five-step ABCDE approach to help us to become more optimistic about situations that have made us anxious, or where we are about to confront situations that do the same:

A = Adversity
B = Beliefs
C = Consequences
D = Disputation
E = Energization

The first step is to write down the **adverse** situation that you have experienced. Then write down the reasons or attributions that you **believe** caused that particular event to take place. In the next stage you look at some of the **consequences** of those particular attributions. This is especially important as we look at the subject of anxiety. The consequences are likely to be avoidance of similar situations in the future because of anxiety about a similar set of circumstances recurring. (We may give up if we are in the middle of a particular activity. These anxieties and fears can be paralyzing if we decide never to encounter similar situations in the future and this can be particularly so if these situations are fairly common in every day life.) The next stage is to challenge (**dispute**) the preconceptions you made about those anxieties and ask:

• Is my reaction (the consequences) really justified?
• Are my beliefs real, imagined or based on half-truths?
• Why should I spend so much time attached to negative beliefs when they are damaging me?

- Am I creating the very circumstances I wish to avoid? The self-fulfilling prophecy?
- If my experience was real and justified, what steps could I take next time to reduce the possibility of repeat?
- What strengths can I use to increase my chances of success?

After disputation we arrive at **energization**. Having identified positive actions to take, the next step is to put these into practice. We use this model in a practical sense in the chapter entitled 'Work: Why has it become my life?', where we apply it to the anxiety-inducing fear of making a presentation.

You can create your own ABCDE chart for those adverse situations you have had to confront yourself using the template below.

A Adversity	
B Beliefs	
C Consequences	
D Disputation	
E Energization	

It should be pointed out that pessimism can also be used as positive weapon against anxiety. In a number of cases, our pessimism and the anxiety it causes are well justified. To illustrate the point, many of us will have gone through financial problems in our lives and, as a result, will have looked to the future with a degree of pessimism. We become anxious about feeding and clothing ourselves, going out for a drink with friends (because we can't really afford it), or even treating ourselves to one or two little luxuries. How do we react to the pessimistic outlook? Well, we can just accept this as our place in the world. Or we can say to ourselves that we will do our best to avoid the pessimistic circumstances we envisage by taking positive actions – taking on an extra job, applying for a new, better-paid one, reducing expenditure or chopping the store and credit cards up into little pieces and having a ceremonial burning!

(x) Your survival can bring fulfilment
Meaning in survival
So Bill Bryson's lichens have got it right after all! Getting through life gives many people in this world all the meaning they could ever need. Readers in India will know very well the huge differences in wealth between the affluent middle classes in Bangalore and Mumbai and the appalling poverty that pervades in this awakening economic giant. Readers in Rio de Janeiro will be aware of the juxtaposition of the wealthy and the ghetto *favelas*. But survival, and the meaning attached to it, can exist in previously comfortable places that have been pulled apart by war, such as Kosovo. Indeed, few remember that Lebanon, and Beirut in particular, were once leisure paradises. The switch from attaching meaning to our comfortable lives to attaching meaning to subsequent survival can be remarkably close to many people in the world, and indeed to many potential readers of this book.

Meaning can be created through survival. Indeed, for many people in the world it has to be. But that survival can be performed with dignity, with concern for one's fellow human beings, with morality and with a desire to give of oneself. Easy to write, you might say for the middle-class English writer, comfortably off in his little corner of south-west France! But, having seen the way in which many, though not all, of the Kosovar people, for example, are attempting to rebuild their country, I would say that their lives are every bit as full of meaning as those of readers in the UK, Australia or Germany.

Longevity is desirable when we consider the experiences that it can give to someone. Once, when travelling on a truck on the poor roads of former Soviet state Georgia for what seemed like hours, I wondered what kept the old peasant farmers going. The answer was that they probably found as much meaning in their lives as you and I do. I was attaching my cultural conditioning to their lives.

So who was right among the psychology giants we featured in this chapter? Academics are good at telling us about meaning and how important it is, but perhaps this is a motivating factor among those who rarely are exposed to the millions who get all the meaning they could need from a nightly dose of *EastEnders*. Perhaps sometimes it pays just to enjoy the here and now, like the Georgian farmer and the *EastEnders* watcher. Sometimes. But perhaps not all the time.

Can you find true happiness?

In my opinion, what we pursue above all else is some kind of happiness or contentment, and that because we want increasingly 'happiness now', we kid ourselves that many of the things that we throw into the partial vacuum will fill the free space and create that happiness. Happiness can give our life meaning. In the past many of us would have gone through a greater range of emotional experiences than we now do (infant mortality, the threat of disease, the struggle to find food and to clothe ourselves and to have adequate shelter, and so on) and in that sense we had all the meaning we could possibly want. Just to survive was a major success. The struggle for survival filled the possibility of a vacuum.

With a longer life now much more likely, but with the desire for a life with meaning beyond struggle, we seek a higher sense of satisfaction, which is our happiness. When surveys seem to indicate that people refer to the 1950s as 'happier times', I wonder if they just meant a simpler time, post-war, when the fact that one had survived and some material progress had been made were enough to make one happy. It is a theme we look at in the final chapter.

What you can do

Sometimes we don't know that something is good until it is taken away from us – particularly if it's something simple. Can you draw up a list of the things you make assumptions about, but which would reduce your happiness if they were removed? Imagine if you didn't have them. How might you feel?

Try not to take for granted the often assumed but simple things that give pleasure and add great value to our lives.

CONSUMING:

Why do I need all this stuff?

The more I eat, the more empty I feel.

Modern post-industrial societies are not 'sick', as some prophets of doom suggest. But it is clear that one of the central causes of groundless anxiety is that we find that we are choosing to fill the existential gaps in our lives with things that add little value or meaning to them (see the preceding chapter). In this chapter we explore one of those 'fillers' – the need to consume. Few of us would deny that we over-consume. Our lives are full of 'stuff' – some of it essential, some of it less so. Clearly, if all this 'stuff' made us happier or attached greater value to our lives, the need to consume excessively would have a purpose.

However, the anxiety we create in ourselves by the need to consume is, for the most part, self-inflicted – albeit because we come under intense pressure in our daily lives to have and consume more. Indeed, the epidemic has now reached the point where all but the strongest are now prey to feelings of inadequacy and perceived low status if they do not conform to the consuming conventions of the post-industrial economies of which they are a part.

In this chapter we look at four examples of the kind of problems we are up against. Thankfully, there are a number of positive actions available to us that can take us in a more rational, questioning direction. These solutions follow the four problems.

Problem one: The 'feeding frenzy'

In the early 21st century, many of us are judged by our buying choices. Not only that, but many of us are defining ourselves by those choices too. The desire to have more, and to work more so that we can have even more, has taken on crazy dimensions. As an extreme example of how this desire to possess and consume has overtaken rational thinking, I tell the story of how a huge fight broke out at the recent opening of an IKEA furniture superstore in Edmonton, England.

The thousand-strong throng of people who were waiting for the midnight opening to snap up early bargains descended on the entrance at the witching hour. (One person had even made a 200-mile round trip from Birmingham to secure a sofa for £40.) Fighting then began over who had claimed certain bargains first. The violent clashes started even before the store's doors opened. Somehow, the press, in their ensuing reports of the incident, managed to turn this into a story about how IKEA hadn't laid on enough security guards at the entrance – as though the fighting masses were not responsible for their own actions.

Imagine the build-up of anxiety as our shoppers psych themselves up for the frenzy and the potential 'horror' of missing their much-anticipated purchase. And imagine the scene itself, with raised blood pressure, complete loss of sense of reason and perspective, and the risk of physical injury. We can, perhaps, understand the near riots that occur when a food delivery truck arrives with food for the starving in a famine-wracked country in Africa. But in the fifth richest country in the world? We have forever fought over basic needs (and may do so again if water becomes scarce), but to fight over superfluous wants is new. However, if we ever wanted evidence that this 'feeding frenzy' instinct exists, it was present that night in its worst manifestation.

Problem two: I am what I consume

In his book *Liquid Life*, sociologist Zygmunt Bauman captures the zeitgeist very well when he writes about our need to consume: 'All human beings are, and always were, consumers, and the human concern with consumption is not news.' But he warns that the problem, and perhaps one of the great changes that has befallen us in the last hundred years, is a society that now '(judges) its members primarily, or even exclusively, as consumers' and 'judges and evaluates its members mostly by their consumption-related capacities and conduct'.

Bauman suggests that we are now defined by our buying choices. I would add that the extreme language we use in connection with potential buying choices defines how our sense of priorities has changed. For example, few would equate the word 'love' with wall tiles, but I recently saw it used by a stylist in a home-care magazine as she described herself 'falling in love with' some bathroom tiles that she just had to have. When we refer to the 'tiger in your tank' and the 'terror in your toilet bowl', is it any wonder, too, that over time we create a whole barrel load of false anxieties based on domestic 'evils' hiding round every corner that have to have a 'solution'?

Problem three: The information generation – 'the good, the bad and the ugly'

Things are about to become a lot more challenging for us. Neuroscientists at UCLA are just about to complete an atlas of the human brain. The process is known as neuro-imaging, and part of the research is beginning to unearth why the limbic system, which is responsible for 'emotions', will often override our rational side when we make decisions. Neuro-imaging is already being extended into 'neuro-economics', where corporations will be able to assess what it is that makes us choose to buy a particular car, or decide what we are going to have for lunch – significant only, of course, for those parts of the world's population who can afford to have a car or have a choice about what they are going to eat.

And it is exactly these choices that are providing us with a conundrum. It seems that, at least where the average consumer is concerned, progress wears two hats – one that could be labelled 'great value' and a second marked 'abuse'. These technological advances will help us peer into our brains, but will also allow others to do the same thing.

Mapping the human brain will help us to understand many critical mental health issues – but what's interesting is that, the more we know about mental health, the more of us seem to have mental health problems. We may be creating technology that helps us to understand what makes us tick, but we're using it in such a way that it has the opposite effect. The medical establishment is excited about this development and it certainly should be. But just as excited is the advertising industry as it foresees a time when it is able to direct advertising at certain parts of the brain prone to making emotional and less rational choices about consumption. We could even see bespoke advertising being tailored to very small groups, or even individuals.

It was always said that the internet (which I maintain is the greatest invention in my lifetime) and computer advancements would allow us to know far more about our world and particularly about those who govern us. But it also means 'they' can watch 'us'. As an example – when my copy editor emailed me her first edit of my last book, she used the 'track changes' function in Microsoft Word, so that I could clearly see what she was changing, what she had deleted, and so on. But I was also able to see on exactly which day and at exactly what time she had made each change. If I had been so inclined, I could have seen when she had a one-hour break – perhaps to have her lunch – and could make assumptions about what she might have been doing when there appeared to be 20-minute gaps in her editing work. It occurred to me that, at some point in the near future, I will be able to *know* what she did with her 'down' time rather than hypothesizing.

With so much of our personal work, exploration and discovery being done via the internet, and with so much of that now being monitored, we will very soon be bombarded with tailored advertising and with calls to consume way beyond current imaginable levels. We have only just begun. To the next generation this will seem normal. To this generation it sounds horrifying.

Problem four: Consumption is progress?

In *Afflenza: The all-consuming epidemic,* author John De Graaf writes of the experiences of anthropologist Allen Johnson as he returned to Los Angeles after studying the Machiguenga tribe, hunter-gatherers in the Amazon rainforest in Peru. On his return, Johnson recalled walking down a supermarket aisle filled completely with cake mixes and wondering, 'Is this really progress?'

The solution

Some of us become anxious if we don't have the possessions we crave, or the money to pay for them, and don't challenge the cycle of thinking where we can't see beyond the need to possess. For many of us, the problem of over-consuming can 'short-circuit' a truly meaningful existence. So what steps can we take to gain control of our spending and consumption habits? How we can we personally overcome some of the problems identified in this chapter? Here are four ways you might like to consider.

(i) Ask yourself – 'Can I choose to opt out altogether?'

DJ, travel journalist and style guru Robert Elms recently wrote an amusing piece in *GQ* magazine where he justified why he didn't have a mobile phone. He said that, for example, when he is having lunch with a friend, he is doing just that – he is not 'in the office'. He sees the mobile as some sort of 'personal tracking device', which allows anyone to locate you, no matter where you are, and find out what you are doing. There seems to be no escape unless you make a very conscious effort to do so. It is not uncommon to see a group of friends sharing a drink in a bar, and for all of them to be texting people outside their immediate circle. Of course, none of them is communicating with each other in any meaningful sense.

Robert Elms sees not owning a mobile phone as a challenge. I experimented with living without one for six months until I started to feel that I might be losing work as a result – a critical factor for someone who is self-employed. I felt that one or two of my clients were questioning my credibility because I didn't have one, so I decided to rejoin the 21st century and get one (although I did opt against choosing one that took photos, sends email, and so on).

There is so much pressure to conform to convention and fashion that we can see it as damaging not to carry a mobile phone. Robert Elms is successful in what he does, and colleagues and friends probably see his choice as an endearing personality quirk. This may be much harder for those who are still trying to find their way in the world or for those who lack confidence. It is much more difficult to make choices about how much paraphernalia we need in our lives when we feel that we may lose out as result.

Of course, owning a mobile phone is not a true consumerist terror. But the pressure to own so much additional gadgetry is. We can ask if we really do need all this stuff.

What you can do

We are always able to make choices. Ask yourself the following questions, and give yourself honest answers: 'How much do I really need, or even want, this or that gadget?', 'Is peer pressure influencing my desire for possessions?', 'Am I buying this because a lot of suggestive advertising is pushing me into believing that I am not a part of the human race unless I have it?' And the biggest question of all – 'How am I going to pay for it?' More debt, more credit?

(ii) Cut out the junk

Have you ever looked at the ingredients of a packet of breakfast cereal? The manufacturers will tell you that the cereal contains wonderful things like thiamine, riboflavin, folic acid and an endless list of vitamins. And then we look down the list further and see that our cereal is also 30–40 per cent sugar, contains a large amount of salt and is of course highly processed. Many breakfast cereals are junk foods masked with some things that make us feel that we are ingesting a product that is good for us.

The danger here, and we use this as a metaphor for life, is that we use the fortification as an antidote or conscience reliever to the junk – 'I have had my daily dose of the good bit, so now I can indulge as much as I like.' What we never do is address the issue of the junk in our lives, be it food or the superfluous things we buy in order to make us feel better. In fact the uptake of these instant gratifications can be enjoyable and occasionally healthy, but increasing the regularity creates its own problems.

These sudden bursts of pleasure are of course unsustainable, even from hour to hour, and we find ourselves needing the next injection of instant gratification to get us back to that momentary (in the context of our lives) high we had before. It's a bit like that mild euphoria you feel after about one and a half glasses of wine. You want to sustain it, so you have another glass, though the effect is not quite the same, and then another. The original feeling becomes elusive because it has no depth or sustainability to it.

Some might argue that 'that which gives me pleasure makes me happy'. But perhaps we need to distinguish between two types of pleasure here. The pleasure of seeing children and grandchildren developing and finding their way in the world is a long-term and sustainable pleasure. A one-night stand with the promise (rarely delivered) of 'get-me-off-the-ceiling' sex is based around the pursuit of instant pleasure. The latter has its benefits but these are likely to be very short-term and unsustainable. For those who regularly pursue one-night stands, the sex itself has become almost like a drug. Maybe fantastic the first time, but decreasingly so the more we access it. In this situation, people often play the numbers game – they know that every so often the experience will be gratifying, so they keep going until sexual 'bingo' is called.

What you can do

This is not an advocation of some form of new puritanical lifestyle! Impulses and gratitousness can have psychological benefit if they are not overindulged. But for many of us they are the only way in which we choose to add any meaning to our lives. Freud believed, as we saw in the preceding chapter, that the 'will to pleasure' was a powerful psychological driving force, but we are all intelligent enough to recognize that a life one-dimensionally based around gratuitous pleasure will create an emotional and spiritual void.

You are also intelligent enough to learn to enjoy your impulses, but to not become a slave to them. Look to find other things that can emotionally and spiritually sustain you.

(iii) Don't believe everything you read!

In the space of three months, one national newspaper in the UK managed to feature stories around all of the following issues:

- Divorce, dyeing one's hair, having big breasts, working long hours and sleeping with the light on can all cause heart disease.
- Cancer can be prevented by eating tomatoes, mushrooms, sauerkraut and eggs, taking folic acid, owning a dog, or by drinking herbal tea and pomegranate juice.
- Sunbathing can both cause and help prevent cancer.
- Mammograms can both cause and help prevent cancer.
- Curry can help prevent Alzheimer's disease.
- Spinach is the secret to keeping you slim.
- Eggs are the new 'superfood'.

This is just a précis of some of the 'health' stories run in many publications (it is not meant to pick on the one that ran them), and is not untypical of the relentless barrage of mixed messages we are confronted with every day.

No wonder we are anxious. How might a woman feel if she is having a mammogram? Or what might readers of this newspaper think if they were contemplating a holiday in the sun? Will there be people out there drinking far more pomegranate juice than is good for them? Or devouring curries every night because of what they read. You bet there will.

What you can do

The gurus of positive thinking suggest that cynicism is not a healthy state of mind. But in a world where we are sent such relentless, mixed and sensationalist messages about our well-being, a healthy dose of cynicism will serve you very well. If a survey suggests a particular course of action that appeals to you, find out who paid for the survey first. If a news article suggests a change in behaviour that you may wish to make, read some opposing arguments and form a balanced judgement for yourself.

Of course, most scare stories can be placed in the bin, but occasionally something comes along that could change our life for the better. The best course of action is to resist impulsiveness and to educate yourself further before undertaking any significant lifestyle changes.

(iv) Exercise self-control when it comes to money

One of the many downsides of the consumerist age is the high level of personal debt we now carry. Those age-old stigmas of bankruptcy and debt are slowly disappearing as we herald a new era where it's now socially acceptable to owe tens of thousands of pounds (or euros or dollars) as long as the value of the house just about covers the debt. But really it is not fine to have multiple credit and store cards, and loans that we are struggling to pay back. Anxiety about personal finances is a huge blight on the health and well-being of many citizens in post-industrial economies.

What you can do

Managing money is about exercising CONTROL (one of the crucial seven 'C's). We are in control only when we have successfully learned to 'let go' psychologically of the things we cannot control and to exercise a positive approach to the things we can. There are a number of money-management controls we can put in place that won't take away all the pleasure we get from healthy consumption (this is not about being a killjoy), but which will allow us to keep control of our personal financial circumstances:

- Budget on a weekly and monthly basis, and make a realistic assessment of what you can afford to spend on impulsiveness and leisure – if anything at all.
- Tell yourself that you will buy only what you can afford to buy.
- Consider putting a small sum aside each month for emergencies. At the end of the year, if the kitty has grown, you can continue to save or else use it for impulse buys. (The joy of spending money on something you have worked to save for often exceeds the joy of spending on impulses that put you deeper in debt.)
- Consider having a debit card only. This gives you the same buying flexibility as a credit card without the need to go into deep debt.
- If you must use a credit card, pay back what you owe each month. If this is a struggle, cut the card in half: you cannot afford to own one – it is as simple as that.
- Ceremonially burn all credit card applications that arrive in the post as a symbolic reminder of the dangers of heading deeper into debt.

In a later chapter, which looks at anxiety in the workplace, we see how to create a series of 'shell statements', which will provide protection for you and reduce the possibility of circumstances occurring where you become anxious. The shell statement helps us to retain or regain control when we feel ourselves losing it. This shell can work for us in other walks of life too. If, for example, we are bad at managing our own finances (a major source of anxiety for many of us), then the benefit of repeating a series of shell statements to ourselves, such as the following, can add discipline to our actions and reduce subsequent anxieties:

- 'I will only buy what I can afford to buy.'
- 'I will budget every month and keep to that budget.'
- 'I won't hide from my debts and assume they will go away. They won't.'

Those who are very heavily in debt have no choice but to exercise these extreme disciplines. Your behaviour must match directly the shell statements you make. Once you have committed to getting control through your shell statements, exercise that control.

Some readers may well be in very serious debt. The debt will not go away on its own but there are many things you can do and options you can take even if you do not think there are. A number of countries have organizations that have been established to help citizens in financially challenging situations, and who will help you negotiate with creditors. There are many not-for-profit, 'no-fee' credit counselling organizations across the world. An internet search will reveal the nearest one for you. But remember: you should access one that is *genuinely* 'no-fee' and not-for-profit.

What you must *not* do is hide away and believe the problem will disappear. There are many people out there who can help you to help yourself. Take control.

RELATIONSHIPS:

How can they be stronger?

> '*I would like capability to be the core of a humane society but it needs to be accompanied by another culture, one that focuses on a concern for others.*'

Charles Handy, *The Elephant and the Flea*

When I began writing this book, I sent out a short questionnaire to friends and friends of friends asking them about what would make them happy in the future, and what they have observed in others that makes them happy. I thought their responses might prove useful when it came to writing the final chapter on future happiness. What interested me was the number of respondents (there were about 50 in total) who commented on the need for strong relationships with family, friends and colleagues as a route to happiness. By extension, I believe that many of the respondents would agree (and some stated this explicitly) that the lack of strong, fulfilling relationships creates a large gap in people's lives.

To begin this chapter, I have selected a few of the comments I received, which I think illustrate the value that many of us place on good relationships.

> *Being there when my family needed me (over the last nine years I had often been absent) and dedicating the best part of myself to them and to my friends, even when I was in extreme difficulty myself. It makes me very happy not to put*

my problems before the ones of others. Mine can wait most of the time if there's someone else who is in a more difficult condition.

Anna, Italy

Having a coffee with an old friend, visiting your close cousin – in our country that is usually someone that you've grown up with – having a wonderful time. Going on a trip with your father and sharing your thoughts with him. All this can serve as an energizer for anyone.

Arlind, Kosovo

People, when they start a relationship, tend to believe that it will bring happiness, and so spend more time on that relationship without objectively thinking that it might change, or that the person involved might one day change. As does everything else in this life, people change and relationships change. Unless we are mentally prepared to accept that fact, we will become unhappy when the changes take place.

Lionel, Sri Lanka

My sister and brother-in-law, after nine years of marriage, decided finally to have a child. During the holidays I had an opportunity to see my brother-in-law lie on the floor with his three-month-old son as they smiled, laughed and stared at one another. A man filled with love and happiness in seeing his child so excited, and a young baby, with no cares, just enjoying life itself. That's what happiness and life is all about.

Wendy, USA

I think that the individuals who appear to be most happy are part of a group of people who support each other, and who respect each other. I have seen this in families, and also in groups of friends. A balance in the group relationship was always present, and no one felt threatened. Everyone realized their own worth.

Lorna, UK

When a team has been through a challenge and has succeeded by supporting each other and they have achieved their goals.

Helen, UK

Creating a family of my own, with a man who is very much like me. Creating close and solid relationships with other like-minded people.

Edona, Kosovo

These are strong sentiments that I suspect few of us would disagree with. And yet many of us fail to build the relationships that would make our lives richer. In this chapter we will look at some of the reasons why this is the case, and what we can do to build better relationships. Some of us have trouble making friends because of shyness, so we will look at how we can overcome this through a systematic process.

There are times in our lives when we resist the very thing we need. Teenagers, finding their place in the world and seeking independence, reject the support they need, often because the offerer, although well intentioned, does not have the sensitivity required to make the intervention an appropriate one. But we are all aware of the well-publicized stories of self-harm, eating disorders and drug abuse that indicate the need for sensitive guidance. Sensitivity is a core emotional skill in the building of relationships. In this chapter we will look at some of the other skills that can help us do this, including empathy, forgiveness, praise and the avoidance of 'emotional hijacking'.

The challenges we face

It might be useful to understand some of the challenges we face to building strong relationships in the 21st century. Here are some of them.

Breaking up is hard to do

If the branches of a tree can be seen as the healthy manifestation of our ability to be happy and to deal with anxiety – and we can all have healthy branches – then strong relationships are likely to be the roots.

But marital breakdown, family disputes, dysfunctional work teams, broken friendships and a general lack of respect from and to people we come into contact with engender distress and unhappiness for those who have to live through these experiences.

Divorce is a rising problem, with between 30 and 40 per cent of married couples in western societies likely to separate. One school of thought says that we should work harder at preserving our marriages and that there are valuable 'tools' to help us do this. Another says that we should look to remove ourselves quickly from relationships that cause overwhelming anxiety, because that anxiety will never fully disappear while the cause of it is still there. Both are easier said than done. And the advice is often contradictory. Pick up one book and it will suggest that XYZ approach works with children, for example. Pick up another and it will suggest a different solution.

There is no cast-iron conventional wisdom that will always help you do the right thing in human relationships. But there are a series of emotional skills that give us the best chance of building relationships that are mutually beneficial and that last. We look at these a little later in the chapter.

Are you talking to me?

The feeling of being 'alone in public' is rarely more obvious than when you're sitting on a train and looking around at all your fellow passengers who, with headphones plugged into their MP3 players, seem tuned out of this world and into their own. This is a tough one,

I admit. I love my music as much as, if not more than, most, but I increasingly find myself disconnecting with people when my listening is confined to my headphones rather than to the world beyond it. We are, of course, terrified of anyone striking up a conversation with us in public. We assume that they are begging, that mentally they might not be quite 'there', or that an unwelcome chat-up has commenced. And so the headphones go on and the message 'DO NOT TALK TO ME' is broadcast. This mindset can perhaps trace its roots to press-led scare stories, which make us believe that any approach from a stranger is to be avoided.

And then we have what comedian and writer Ben Elton calls the 'gottahaveadoubleseat' phenomenon. Not only are the headphones on, but you think, 'I don't really want anyone to sit next to me either,' so you plonk your bag down next to you, or manoeuvre your body in such a way that it is covering one and a half seats. Ideally you want to have the seats opposite you too, so you stretch your legs out far enough to cover the space in front of those seats. And because you are sending out the signal that you are not available for conversation, the person who wants a seat is loath to ask you to move your bag, legs or posterior. You now have the exquisite four feet of personal space but, I would argue, very little else.

So where has the desire to build an outdoor cocoon come from? Clearly, for many, the fear of social interaction has been played up by the press to such an extent that many of us have developed anxieties about the kinds of people we are likely to come across. Are all the normal people in cars, and the socially undesirable (plus me) confined to public transport where, 'God forbid', we may have to sit next to someone, or, worse still, actually talk to them? Doesn't it feel strange when we hear two strangers meeting and talking comfortably during a train journey? Try striking up a conversation on a train these days and people think you are mad or lonely, and therefore have something lacking in your personality.

I may have gone to an extreme to make the point about fear of social interaction in 'the wild', but I am sure many readers will identify with this. Scare stories have made us anxious about any interaction beyond our cosy bubbles. Where we do interact, it tends to be with those with whom we feel we have an affinity (in terms of colour, social background, age, and so on).

There is a difference too between 'being alone in public' and enjoying, for example, the 'socializing anonymity' that living in a city can bring. It is a paradox that one can be more anonymous in a city of seven million people than when living in the country. 'Being alone in public' concerns itself with alienation from the community – a different feeling altogether and an all-too-real experience for many of us. How can we try to feel that we are part of something when we feel completely disconnected?

We now look at some of the approaches we can take in building relationships. We begin with some of the helpful emotional skills, continue with approaches that will make us more of a social animal, and end with that great cause of anxiety – dealing with a fear of social situations.

(1) Building relationships – the vital 'emotional skills'

'Human beings relate to each other not simply externally, like two billiard balls, but by the relations of the two worlds of experience that come into play when two people meet.'

R. D. Laing, *The Mystification of Experience*

The strength of your relationships with others is likely to be influenced by your relationship with yourself. Possessing a degree of self-awareness and an outward-looking perspective that allows you to project your personality on to the world will impact substantially on your relationships with others. In this section, we look at the emotional skills involved in building relationships. These emotional skills can be learned if they don't come naturally to you, but they provide the nourishment that is needed in order to build healthy relationships.

Show empathy

When we empathize with someone, we imagine what it might be like to be that other person. Daniel Goleman, in his book *Emotional Intelligence*, suggests that this is really about reading the feelings of others. He expands this by saying: 'Empathy builds on self-awareness. The more open we are to our own emotions, the more skilled we will be in reading feelings.'

We pay more attention to our feelings and emotions if we deem them to be important. In past generations it was seen as unmanly to be in tune with one's emotions with the result that, for example, many fathers struggled to have any kind of warmth in their relationships with their children. In the workplace, traditionally an area where convention demands the suppression of emotion, relationships with colleagues rarely go beyond the superficial unless we have worked with someone for a considerable period of time, and have got to know them, or at least got to know their work persona.

Increasingly we see emotions and the reading of them as important: teachers working with pupils; friends who want to be real friends; managers who want to understand if what is being said is what is really felt by those they manage; men/women wanting to empathize with their partner who comes home after 'a bad day at the office', and so on. These are all areas in which emotional understanding will serve as the basis for a stronger relationship. So what do we look out for when we try to read emotions? Here are some suggestions:

Body language: fidgeting, crossing and uncrossing the legs, touching parts of the face, a particular interest in a part of the body (digging fingernails, for example).

Voice: timid or overly loud; cracked.

Eyes: lack of, or over-emphasized, eye contact; redness.

Language: passive (self-diminishing – for example: 'It was nothing' (when getting praise), 'I am hopeless'; aggressive (strong language, bringing up people's perceived inadequacies); reluctance to talk.

Physiognomy: red face, sweating, emphasized veins, flared nostrils.

We can also spot some of these signs in ourselves as we learn to read our own emotions better. Many of us unconsciously leak signals about what we are really thinking and feeling, even though the words we use might be suggesting a different thought pattern.

Empathy is a lot more than reading signals in a cold way. It is about understanding and seeing the world from the perspective of the other person. But these signals will help us in the first to step to making deeper connections. As we see in the section on sensitivity, below, we also have to know when to back off. Empathetic skills are also about knowing when to 'be there' and when to withdraw. It's a bit like the salesperson in a shop who knows when to offer assistance and advice and when to leave you to browse. Some of us like to keep our distance some or most of the time. The empathetic person understands this.

Accommodate the 'hot planets' of others

When we looked at 'hot planets' in the first chapter, we saw the advantage in understanding our own 'hot planets' – that is the combination of emotions and knowledge concerning particular things that provokes different reactions in us when challenged. (Readers who have jumped to this section may find it useful to refer back to the explanation of 'hot planets' as a self-understanding exercise on page 16.)

In building relationships, we need to appreciate that others have 'hot planets' too. If you have a large planet close to your sun (ego) called, say, religion, and you meet someone who has a similar planet in size and proximity to their sun (ego) as you, this is no guarantee that you will connect. You may have totally different perspectives on the same subject – witness, for example, the huge internal conflicts within Christianity or Islam. Our tolerance of the 'hot planets' of others – and the uniqueness of their world view – will determine how far we will go in developing long-term relationships. No one will have the same match as you. Whether it is friendship or love you seek, waiting for someone like you can be a fruitless search. Like the real planets, our own planets are ever-changing.

We all change, and as Lionel from Sri Lanka said in his reply to my questionnaire at the beginning of this chapter, we have to learn to accommodate the change or the relationship or friendship will stall.

I recall writer and broadcaster Charles Handy once saying that he had been married twice, but to the same woman. Recognizing each other's changes in wishes and aspirations as they moved into late middle-age, he and his wife 'renegotiated' their marriage – although I doubt it was done in the formal way that the word 'renegotiate' suggests.

In building new relationships, you may find it helpful to consider the following:

- Make it part of the fun of life to enjoy the company of people who are not like you. You will learn far more than you will from surrounding yourself with like-minded thinkers.

- Confident people who struggle to form strong relationships may do so because they find it hard to accommodate others. For example, if your confidence is born out of your belief in your intelligence, then you might believe that you are right *because* you are intelligent. As a result, you might not accommodate those who are 'wrong' (and therefore unlike you). This is one of the bases for arrogance.

- In disagreement or argument, don't get hung up about what you disagree on. Build from the strongest point, which is what you agree on.

- Searching for like-minded people is one of the great hindrances to growing relationships. On that basis I would not be capable of connecting with even my own daughters because they are already very different from me, and from each other.

- Be cautious about forming snap judgements about people. Often these judgements are made in the heat of the moment, and cloud our ability to look for further signs that would confirm or, more likely, challenge that perspective.

Control the temptation to overreact

Sometimes we let emotion hijack reason. If our reactions to injustice (real or imagined) are highly emotive and, as a consequence, we are verbally or physically aggressive, we are clearly not in control of ourselves. Alcohol, drug or substance abuse can lead to heightened emotions and inappropriate and sometimes dangerous behaviour. Not a healthy way to build lasting relationships.

This isn't exclusively the preserve of those prone to abuses that alter our ability to think rationally. Our brain, through evolutionary processes, is wired to give swift reaction to danger as a form of defence. However, we can learn through understanding the effects of highly emotive reactions that considered, rational reactions will usually get a more productive outcome (unless the danger is very real and immediate). The key here is that we have to possess the desire to learn about responses. Those who wonder why the world seems to dislike them might like to consider the fact that they don't give it much of a chance to like them. People in this group reinforce this way of thinking by seeing their emotional behaviour (aggressive, passive, and so on) as 'normal' and then they don't question why they get the reactions they do.

Develop sensitivity

In this section we return to a theme we started at the beginning of the chapter – the need for sensitivity in building relationships, particularly where others are prone to their own sensitivities. Parents, for example, will recognize the anxiety that their children generate and the need for a sensitive approach. In their book *Happy Families*, authors Bill Lucas and Dr Stephen Briers suggest a number of ways of parenting teenage children. They suggest some 'Don'ts' (and one 'Do'):

Don't talk 'hip'.
Do dress your age.
Don't show photos of them to their friends.
Don't swear.

Don't drink too much.
Don't make jokes about sex.
Don't try to be cool in front of their friends.

The idea of trying to be cool is tempting, but not advisable!

This list has been drawn from the experiences of many parents with teenage children. It has been developed through a process of understanding the world of teenagers – where empathy is key – and adapting our behaviour accordingly. To be sensitive to the needs of others, particularly those friends, partners, colleagues, and so on, who may need our help, sensitivity born out of empathy is important. Relationships work both ways, and at times when you are anxious you will need the help of others too. The more you give, the more you are likely to get in return.

When we are in a position to help others our approach is crucial. Recently I have had to respond to a call for help from a friend who needed me. In that situation it was very difficult not to say straight out what the problem was (even though I suspected that I knew). A good approach in a case like this is to discuss the issue in such a way that the other person recognizes the causes themselves ('What do you think might be the cause of this?') and sees that they have options ('What options are open to you?'). It is tempting to say, 'What you need to do is…' This is inadvisable as it gives the impression that you are solving the other person's problems for them. People act best on that which they have realized for themselves.

Each of us is unique, with a distinct set of anxieties (although some of these will be shared), and we should seek to build a rapport that reflects this uniqueness – whether it is with teenage children, friends or colleagues.

Show forgiveness

'Forgive and forget,' the old cliché says. One of these is realistic – the other much less so. It takes many years to blank out of our mind what we believe to be a wrong, but we have the capacity to forgive the person who did it. There are of course levels of wrong. Pope John

Paul II meeting and forgiving his would-be assassin is one thing, and would be beyond the radar for most of us. A friend or colleague who lets us down is another. We may feel a little less about that friend or colleague for a time and we can and should make our friend aware, in a sensible non-emotive manner, that we felt let down. But we should also, without being patronizing, make it clear that we are moving on and still see them as a good friend or colleague.

If you struggle with this idea, look at it the other way round. How might a life bearing grudges and vendettas feel? Sadly a number of us seem to do just this, and we can easily slip into a mindset that says that the world, and the people in it, are against us. We become anxious about building relationships in the future because of it. But if we cannot find it in us to forgive, we run the risk of letting an extremely damaging emotion drag us down.

Of course, if the person repeats the wrong after we have shown forgiveness, we are presented with a challenge. Followers of the Christian faith would say that part of the test of faith is to have an endless capacity for forgiveness in the way that Christ did. Others might say that to forgive is one thing, but to have that forgiveness abused is another. You will have to make your own judgement as to how far your capacity to forgive stretches, but being able to forgive removes a degree of negativity from your life. One should not, however, be naïve about the weaknesses of others! We should not be taken advantage of.

Give altruistically

In line with what most thinkers agree are the true traits of the less anxious, we must understand that these emotional skills are not about the selfish pursuit of personal enrichment. There can be a higher good about what we do from which we might personally benefit, but this should not provide the motivation to do so. The 19th-century Utilitarians (and the founders of 20th-century 'liberalism') based their thinking around the philosophies of Jeremy Bentham and John Stuart Mill, who argued passionately in their writing for what they called 'the greatest good for the greatest number'. Personal liberalism was inextricably linked to the well-being and happiness of others too.

Learning to give to others with no expectation of personal gain is one of the highest, perhaps the highest, of all emotional skills. In fact, many of us do this already – from the things we are encouraged to do as children (for example, helping an old lady across the road) to the huge rise in charitable donations, to the giving of blood. And few of us would deny that we don't feel a lot better as a result. We get something valuable in return, even though we did not seek it.

Wouldn't you rather be remembered by how much you gave rather than how much you took?

Avoid the continual need for praise

When we are young we are taught to seek approval. When we get it – praise perhaps for doing something good – we feel good, so naturally we seek more of it. And so the spiral continues. This is no bad thing. It is valuable in helping us to learn right from wrong and to recognize danger. However, having learned that approval makes us feel good as a child, we can find that, even though we are doing well, we get less praise in adulthood than we had before. On workplace stress courses that I run, participants often tell me that few managers give praise and thanks for good work and, as a consequence, they, as employees, can start to believe that what they do is insignificant. Not long after that, they start to feel that they themselves are insignificant.

When a simple 'Thanks for doing that – you did it really well' would be such a powerful motivator, it's surprising that it's not done more often in the workplace. And it is equally surprising that we don't see how powerful praise and thanks are in developing relationships. If someone sees that we value them and what they do, their self-esteem is likely to be raised, and they will value us all the more for it. We mutually benefit from our initiating behaviour. One word of warning here – we must be sincere and the actions that gain the praise and thanks must be worthy of it.

(2) Collaboration – that's what friends are for

One of the places we go to last when we feel uncomfortably anxious is perhaps the place we should go to first – to our partners in life. By partners I don't just mean 'other halves' but friends, family and perhaps work colleagues too. Seeing life as a collaborative process in both the good times and the bad provides a valuable 'glue' with which we maintain a healthy connection with the world – even if in the bad times we may not feel like making that connection. This COLLABORATION is a critical element in combating anxiety and is one of the all-important seven 'C's I identified in the introductory chapter. One reason that we are loath to collaborate is that we do not feel comfortable 'showing ourselves up'. We can think of many people in our lives, and I have to say that in my life they mostly seem to be male, who would benefit substantially from sharing their problems, but who believe that to do so shows weakness. People like this are usually very ready to offer advice (but often not in a way that is useful) to others because doing this serves to reassert their 'mental strength'. They may come to us only when they are really desperate.

Our friends, family and work colleagues, but also many people beyond our inner circle, provide a vital, perhaps the *most* vital, way of helping ourselves out of difficulty. Anxieties concerning money, relationships, work and health can be shared because many of us have been through similar experiences. It is also easy to feel embarrassed once you have removed the anxiety, or used it positively. You do not need to be embarrassed. You should feel proud that you got through.

Here is an interesting exercise that does two things:

(i) Helps us to understand how much of the pleasure we gain from life comes from our interaction with others.

(ii) Demonstrates the fact that a proactive approach to relationships provides an escape channel for built-up angst.

If I ask you now to describe what a good day for you might feel like – and I mean things within your power, not things that are based on luck, like winning the lottery – there will be a great diversity of answers, but usually one consistent theme. Write down what a good day for you might be like now, and try to express it in a reasonable amount of detail – probably as more than one 'event' in that day. Perhaps a day spent on the beach, with a gin and tonic on the lounger? A good dinner out with friends after a day's pampering at the health spa, followed by a sensual, sexual experience? Or a good, long breakfast with the newspapers, followed by time at a sports event and an evening with friends at the pub?

Some of us enjoy our own company, and certainly a part of my perfect day would involve being mentally 'alone'. But, of course, as social animals we are never truly alone, and neither do many of us want to be so for any length of time. The enjoyment of a live sports event, even when we choose to go by ourselves, is a shared experience. You wouldn't want to go to a football match and be the only person in the crowd, in the same way you probably wouldn't want to be marooned alone on a desert island with that lounger and gin and tonic. The pleasure we derive from life relies on collaboration, the interaction with our fellow human beings and the sharing of all the good times. Still need convincing? That book that you want to spend all day reading on your 'perfect day' was written by someone else (unless you are truly narcissistic!).

So much for the good times (and don't forget to put the good day on the agenda). If life is a collaboration in the happy times, it is also a collaborative one in the anxious ones. As we saw earlier in this chapter, we sow the seeds of their value to us by our own atti-tude to the people in our world. Strong relationships nourish us in the good times. The collaboration that can help us in the tough times will be nourished by the valuing of relationships in the better ones too.

(3) Join a 'community' – be part of something

The COMMUNITY (another of our seven 'C's) in which you operate – your workplace, town or club – adds meaning to what it is that makes you individually unique. Without being part of a community, you have little concept of your uniqueness because you would have nothing to relate to other than the state of nature. We frequently use character descriptions based around our engagement with our social surroundings – friendly, shy, extrovert, introvert, sociable, withdrawn, and so on. Even words like 'hermit' conjure up a whole personality based around withdrawal from the social community. But having to make a connection with others, in whatever kind of social setting, can lead to a very common condition – what is known as 'social anxiety' and which many readers will identify in themselves as shyness. In the first chapter we looked at the modes of thinking (lack of confidence, enduring a bad experience or having to deal with people we find difficult) that can lead to social anxiety.

Fortunately, although most of us have experienced it to some extent, it rarely goes beyond a mild anxiety. Nonetheless, it is one we could do without, and one that can lead us to avoid certain situations that should be enjoyable. At its worst, however, it can result in our gradual withdrawal from our community.

What the person who suffers from a mild social anxiety may find, if they assess how they get through the challenging situation, is a simple process, well expressed by Gillian Butler in her book *Overcoming Social Anxiety and Shyness*. Here she suggests the use of the 'Forward Search Plan'.

EXERCISE

Begin by expressing something you believe about yourself in social situations, then attach a percentage to it representing the extent to which you believe that statement. So you might pick, for example, 'I am hopeless at workplace drinks receptions', and estimate that this is 75 per cent true. Having done this, you then need to do a 'before-the-event assessment'. This comprises three stages:

1. **Think of a future situation that will be difficult for you.**
   For example: 'I have my company's annual drinks reception for key clients coming up.'

2. **Identify your expectation or prediction (which should fit in with your belief).**
   For example: 'I won't know what to say to anyone. No one will be interested in talking to me. It will be dull. I will end up carrying the drinks all evening as a way of avoiding conversation.'

3. **Formulate the search plan: What should I be looking out for?**
   For example: 'The conversations I have. The people who ask me about me. Whether I am bored. What I physically do.'

Then, after the event, consider the following two questions:

1. **The outcome: What actually happened?**
   For example: 'It went quite well. I did talk to a few people – three of us had a good conversation for quite a while. I did have to find an excuse to get away from one person – we just didn't "click". The two people I had a long conversation with asked me a few questions about my job and seemed genuinely interested. For the most part I didn't think about the time, so I probably wasn't bored. I carried the drinks tray for a while, but I got talking to my "friendly couple" and put the tray down – someone must have taken it.'

2. **What conclusions can I draw from that?**
   For example: 'I did notice that the more I asked a question – any question – the better the conversation, but I do sometimes find it hard to think of things to ask until I get going. I think I maybe have a fear of boredom and awkwardness because of this, and I might want to think about ways of dealing with that.'

In reality we often find that the things that we think are going to be bad aren't nearly as bad as we fear they will be. Finally, we can reassign a new percentage figure to the belief we stated at the beginning. For it to go down to zero would be unrealistic. But a reduction to, say, 50 per cent is a considerable step. It is often our proactive approach that makes the difference. Of course, on paper it sounds easy. But a step-by-step approach, such as the one we have seen here, can make a difference. Perhaps for those who have had a bad social experience it helps to understand that these are entirely normal, and are not a reflection on any social inadequacy on your part. Can you perhaps even learn to laugh about it? Some dark humour often helps.

Conclusion – watering the roots

This chapter has explained how we can build stronger relationships. Those stronger relationships do, among many other things, provide us with a social fabric that can help us when we are anxious. It might be based around the need to share thoughts and feelings with someone or to be around people we can enjoy good times with. And more good times give us a good antidote to anxiety.

To continue the metaphor we used at the beginning, the quality of our relationships provides the roots for a strong and healthy tree. The tree is our quality of life.

WORK:

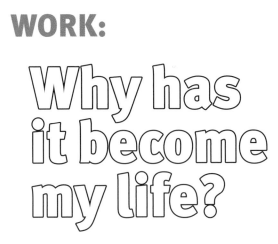

Why has it become my life?

You might not be able to choose the work you do, but you can have the freedom to decide how it is that you are going to do that work.

The ideal state?

In my previous book, *Positive Thinking, Positive Action*, I used workplace psychologist Mihaly Czikszentmihalyi's 'flow' concept to introduce the idea that a job can be far more than just something you do between nine and five. This 'flow' state has been described as the state you get into when you are doing exactly what you want to be doing, and do not want what it is you are doing to end. In fact, thinking about the completion of a task implies that, in this 'flow' state, one is thinking about time, although that is likely to be the last thing on our mind when we are truly engaged.

In my book on positive thinking, I described what the 'flow' state can feel like: 'Sometimes workers are able to engage so freely in their work that they forget that they are actually working. They "flow", moving from Position A to Position B, in an almost ethereal manner, without recourse to extreme emotion or stress, and seem to love what they are doing.'

You might be reading this and asking, 'Who are you trying to kid?' And I wouldn't blame you! When we talk to those who have anxieties in their lives, it is clear that the workplace is a major source of anxiety for many of them. But, actually, many of us do experience this 'flow' state in our work, although these experiences may be infrequent.

Try the following exercise.

EXERCISE

Think back over your working life so far. Can you recall a time when you enjoyed a particular part of your job, even if it was for only 20 minutes? How would you describe how you felt at that time? What made you enjoy it?

It is likely that, during the experience on which you reflected, you were, at least for part of it, in the state of 'flow'. The point being that we do all experience it, even if only rarely, and this makes us believe that our job is worthwhile.

However, the Dalai Lama, in his book *The Art of Happiness at Work*, suggests that 'flow', while highly desirable, is also unsustainable. He says: 'Dealing with one's destructive emotions while at work, reducing anger, jealousy, greed and so on, and practising relating to others with kindness, compassion, tolerance; these are much more stable sources of satisfaction than simply trying to create "flow" as much as possible.'

The answer might come somewhere between the two. It involves identifying the 'best fit' between you and the work you do, so that you can attain the 'flow' state more often, but also gaining a set of emotional and behavioural skills that will give you a sense of serenity while doing that work. And it involves valuing the network of relationships we develop through our work, and the positive emotions that this *can* bring out in us. The Dalai Lama, when asked what he did for a living, replied 'nothing'. Perhaps this is the most highly desirable state of all. When our work is also our leisure – woven into every fibre of our being so that it ceases to be work at all. Fanciful? Perhaps. But not unobtainable.

A good fit for you?

As a follow-on from the previous exercise, and to assess whether your job is a good fit for you, try this exercise.

EXERCISE

Divide a sheet of paper into three columns. In the left-hand column make a list of the kinds of things that you like doing outside the workplace that you have a choice about. This list might include reading, sport, music, holidays, family activities and hobbies. Try to be reasonably specific. In the second column, make a list of how those things make you feel. Hobbies, for example, might make you feel challenged, or give you a feeling that you are learning new things. Sport might bring out the competitor in you, or provide a vehicle for you to strive to achieve particular goals – even if you were under some pressure you would be likely to see the pressure as a positive thing. But your feelings list is also likely to include words like 'relaxed', 'happy', 'calm', 'entertained', and so on.

In the final column, think about your work and how it makes you feel. You may well include positive words, such as 'challenging' and 'excited', but many readers will also list words like 'frustrated', 'anxious', 'angry', 'bored', 'pointless', and so on. It can be easier to connect negative statements with work than positive ones, so do look to include the positive elements too.

Look back at what you've written in the columns. If you have struggled to include items in column one, you may want to consider whether you have enough things going on in your life outside work that help relieve stress and anxiety. The second and third columns are particularly interesting. A commonality between the two suggests that you are in a job that brings out positive emotions in you – that your job is a good fit for you. It should be stated here that even if your job experience is largely positive, you may still have some anxieties connected with that job. This is fine – indeed at a manageable level these anxieties are helpful to us. The trip point occurs where we go from an anxiety bringing out the best in us to it producing an adverse reaction.

A high number of negative statements in column three, or a discord between columns two and three, suggest that there are a number of factors which could be creating stress and anxiety for you in your work. They could include some, or all, of the following:

- You are in a job that does not suit you. Your likes, wants and interests are not served by the role you're in.
- You are not in control of the circumstances surrounding your job. In this situation it can be useful to make a list of the things you *can* control (how you manage your time, for example), and the things you cannot (changing your boss, for instance). It is easy to say that you should not worry about what you cannot change, but to do so is completely wasted energy. (The rest of this chapter looks at some of the areas where you might be able to improve matters.)
- This one is the hardest to say! Is it your attitude? Treating work as something that is inherently bad for you, be it the people you work with and/or the job you do, will help create the perfect self-fulfilling prophecy.

The perfect workplace does not exist!

No matter how much motivational material exists to tell us about the perfect working environment, the ideal workplace does not exist and it probably never will. Our fellow human beings and our own personality traits will see to that. But with a healthy recognition of what causes workplace anxiety, and with some practical tools that we can use to overcome these, the challenges we meet at work can be tamed. It begins with understanding what the causes of workplace anxiety are and to assess if these are making us anxious. So what, more specifically, are the things that cause us anxiety in the workplace? We have no choice about working – indeed many of us want to work, although the conditions that we apply to that, such as not being patronized, being treated with respect, learning new things and being healthily challenged, are important. I feel comfortable in saying that there are around 10 per cent of us who would maximize both our effort and enjoyment in our work no matter what that work entailed (within reasonable bounds, of course). At the other end of the scale we have the 10 per cent or so who seem to be beyond employment, or indeed self-employment.

In the middle we have a huge number of people, perhaps up to 80 per cent of us, who want to do a good job, and who want to be able to enjoy large chunks of our work, but for whom a number of variables have to connect in order for us to do so. These include freedom to do a substantial part of the job in the best way we think fit, to be treated with respect and not to have unreasonable demands placed on us. And, of course, the job has to fit reasonably well with who we are as a person. Of course, the fit is rarely, if ever, perfect. Accepting this can help to reduce the anxiety we may feel about our work, and allow us to come to terms with the fact that what we are doing now may not have been our first choice of career when we left formal education.

Where am I now?

So what are the challenges? What are the things that can create a more anxious environment? We begin with an exercise taken and adapted from Eve Warren and Caroline Toll's *The Stress Workbook*, which gets you to look at your own stress levels. It is a useful starting point because what causes us stress at work will sow the seeds of anxiety about the work we do. One will inevitably lead to the other if we let it. The exercise will provide you with a snapshot of some of the areas that may be causing difficulties for you at work, and will also give you an overall picture of your current stress levels.

EXERCISE

Charting your workplace stress levels

Think about your current job and use the following chart to identify the levels of stress and anxiety you may currently be experiencing in it. You simply need to circle a number on each line that most closely equates to your current experience. So, for example, if you strongly agree with the statement that your 'position is too secure', you might choose to circle 1, 2 or 3. If, however, you feel that your 'position and organization are insecure' you might circle 7, 8 or 9 instead. Somewhere between and your choice might be 4, 5 or 6. When you have done the exercise, add the 12 circled numbers together and you will have a single score of between 12 and 108.

Position too secure. Path predictable and mapped out	1 2 3 4 5 6 7 8 9	Position and organization insecure
Too few demands	1 2 3 4 5 6 7 8 9	Too much to do
Tasks too easy	1 2 3 4 5 6 7 8 9	Tasks too hard
Too quiet	1 2 3 4 5 6 7 8 9	Too noisy
Repetition and lack of variety	1 2 3 4 5 6 7 8 9	Too much variety
Boredom	1 2 3 4 5 6 7 8 9	Many different projects on the go
Too little travelling	1 2 3 4 5 6 7 8 9	Too much travelling
Too little career progression	1 2 3 4 5 6 7 8 9	Fast career track
Too little influence, control or responsibility	1 2 3 4 5 6 7 8 9	Too much influence, control or responsibility
Too little interest or involvement in work	1 2 3 4 5 6 7 8 9	Too much interest or involvement in work
Over-managed	1 2 3 4 5 6 7 8 9	Under-managed
My score: Scale: UNDERSTRESS	12 ... 60 ... 108	OVERSTRESS

A healthy score would be somewhere between 50 and 70 – where there is a balance across what Eve Warren calls 'the pressure points'. Someone who experiences regular stress in their work (where the demands placed on them are overshadowed by their perceived lack of ability to cope with those demands) can easily then become anxious about that work. As we make the connection between our stressed state and the work we do, we start to become anxious about that work and possibly about the effect it is having on us.

Those anxieties can derive from an extensive list including some or all of the following:

- We drive to work and the roads are always full of traffic and slow-moving. So anxiety builds up in us before we even leave home as we anticipate the journey ahead.
- We have an ever-growing and never-ending list of things to do, and we become increasingly anxious about ever getting through the list.
- We feel unchallenged and therefore wearied by the prospect of another day of boredom.
- We have a poor relationship with our boss or with some colleagues, and the prospect of having to make requests or demands or discuss issues with them fills us with apprehension.
- We don't really know how we fit in or how what we do fits into the bigger picture, so we become despondent at the apparent futility of the work we do.
- The possibility of the job changing, or the threat of redundancy or relocation, leads us to fear for our future security and therefore to become anxious.

This is not an exhaustive list, but many of us will have experienced some of these feelings during our working lives.

It is possible to score between 50 and 70 on this chart and to have anomalies in your individual scores – you can answer 1 and 9 alternately and get an apparently middle-ranking 'healthy' score. So do check for clusters of scores. Do you have a number of 8s and 9s or 1s and 2s even though your score is near the 60 mark? If you have a high number of 1s and 2s together with a high number of 8s and 9s that produce a middling score, you may want to examine the specific areas in which you have produced a high 'stress' score or a low 'lack of pressure/challenge' score.

It is also important to make clear that this is only a rough guide. Do not become anxious because your score is a bit over 70 or a bit under 50. Use it as a guide to help you identify where you may be able to release some of the pressure, or, if you are under-challenged, add additional challenges. I have been frequently told by people that they feel under-challenged, and I detect that many of those people tend to be in their 50s. Sadly, employers are not great at presenting new challenges among employees they perceive to be 'on the way to retirement'. In those circumstances, many people I have spoken to report that they overcome this by giving themselves new and invigorating challenges outside the workplace.

What makes us anxious at work?

STUDY

CASE

Jacqueline's story (New York City)

I guess the challenges I face in my job are not untypical and I know that many of my friends and colleagues do not feel so differently. I work in an environment that is connected to some of the world's tougher challenges – war, famine, disease, and so on, and so I guess I wouldn't be doing the job I do if I didn't understand that the challenges are always accentuated.

I work in an environment of chronic change – months of re-structuring with no clear leadership or chain of command at the end of it. My boss left recently too, as did one of my peers and my admin assistant. I've got an intern in the meantime but she goes next month. So you can imagine that one of my biggest challenges is the perennial battle to keep the work done in my department when there aren't the people to do it. It really is a case of one person doing the work of four at the moment.

We all need some appreciation. But I never get a 'We know it's tough – thanks for hanging on in there' from a manager, for example. I do get to hear that external letters of appreciation have come in, but these don't get passed around like they should be. And linked to this is the lack of feedback I get on my work from peers and from management. And sometimes just getting access to decision-makers can be a challenge because the area I work in is seen as low-priority. I get anxious when I think of the effort I will have to put in just to get a meeting with a decision-maker.

This lack of communication presents other obstacles too. We all know the saying 'the goal posts are shifting'. With me it's more a case of the sand shifting beneath me. When I am asked to do something, I often get back: 'Well I don't need this now, I need this instead'. Or: 'That's not what I wanted' or 'That's OK, but I also need this.'

Everything I do seems to be hastily planned, when a little bit more time might enable me to do my best. I get to travel quite a bit – Africa and Asia – and could do so much more in these places if I had the time to plan more effectively. And of course that subject of time relates to my everyday work back at the office too – I just play catch-up all the time.

So what keeps me going in my job?

I do consciously try to focus on the things where I perceive there to be autonomy. Where I can I co-ordinate directly with external people, rather than going through people here at the main office, and I find I build stronger relationships as a result. And by extension I avoid contact where possible with people who have done a lot of rejecting in the past.

I don't necessarily feel anxious about coming in to work in the morning. It's more a sense of failure and frustration that I have been unable to complete some of my most critical tasks and at the lack of control over my work environment. I also try to look out to the river from the office whenever possible to take a mini-chill – watch the tugboats. I also like to channel into my thoughts – my German *grandma was a Russian concentration camp survivor in the Second World War. If she made it through that, I can survive my brilliant idea being shot down or my common-sense approach being dismissed. I also think back to a previous job in Kosovo and all the challenges I experienced there. My job may be stressful these days, but it isn't so bad in the bigger picture. I think it is important to maintain a sense of perspective.*

I take a proper lunch break – seeing friends, meeting new people and colleagues. In the evening I keep an active cultural schedule – movies, plays, dance, and so on. I get a massage every week. I try to take a day off occasionally: I see a film, meet a friend for lunch or dinner, do some things in my apartment or go to some sort of cultural activity – the last one was a photography display. It all helps. I must admit that I have been poor at going to the gym, but I know this helps too, and I do try to go on the weekends! Keeping this balance between work and outside stimulations is important, particularly in tougher jobs like mine.

I just want to be able to work in an enabling environment. So I think it is important to be able to keep a sense of the future and to recognize that there are many things you can do. I like to feel proactive about my future, so I do one action each week regarding a future job. It might be an interview, submitting an application or updating my CV. It helps me realize that there is always escape and it minimizes my feeling of being stuck and out of control.

Restoring 'balance'

Jacqueline's story is realistic. It doesn't tell us that the problems and challenges of the workplace can be transformed immediately. What it does do is to present the kind of difficulties that many readers would, I am sure, identify with, and some strategies that Jacqueline uses to help her though the challenges. Here we look at some of those strategies in greater detail.

Create 'me' time

In the age of long hours and machismo-based work cultures, we can be persuaded that the giving over of your life to your work is a sensible option. We all work hard and, whatever the statistics and experts tell us, it is a fact of life that the successful global economies and indeed the successful careerists work very hard. It becomes imperative that we have some clear boundaries between work and home (or leisure). In Jacqueline's case, she relates how she maximizes the value of her lunch break and her evening time.

Some misguided employers, while not explicitly stating it (because in many places it is illegal), discourage employees from taking lunch. The 'working lunch' has entered the lexicon of business speak. But sitting in a meeting room, eating a lunch we haven't chosen, is not a break. Even in Paris, where the two-hour lunch break used to be commonplace, we hear reports of a grabbed 15-minute sandwich becoming the norm.

It needs to be explicitly stated that we do not work anywhere near our best in the afternoon if we don't get a break at lunchtime. Start half an hour early and finish half an hour later if you have to (and sometimes we do have to), but that one-hour break at lunch is very important for your well-being.

In the first chapter we looked at knowing yourself as a way of combating stress and anxiety. This also applies to the issue of how you work. From personal experience I used to find that my energy levels were at their best in the first part of the day, as apparently is the case with most of us. When really busy, I had no qualms about regularly being at my desk at 7am, but I never worked beyond 5.30pm. I recall being challenged by a manager who questioned my commitment as I left at the same time every day. This manager had no idea I was at my desk at 7am, and was shocked that I actually worked a longer day than he did, even though this manager would leave at around 6.30pm. On stress courses I have run, many participants have said that they enjoy being at work early. Early starters get lots done, with little disturbance, and get precious time to plan their day before it really begins and the phone starts ringing.

What is clear, however, is that we should not feel a compulsion to always start early or finish late because the employer and/or the nature of the job demand it. Getting away from the office at a reasonable time gives us one considerable advantage – we keep work and home life in healthy balance – which takes us into the next point…

Keep a sense of perspective

Work is part of life. It is not life itself. Take the chance now to write down what time you left the office each day last week and what you did afterwards. Many of us struggle to remember because we did not do anything memorable. Our evening is often seen as a preparation for the next day rather than as something to be enjoyed for itself. We spend 80,000 hours of our life on average at work but almost five times that not at work, yet work can take over our non-working existence.

Work is crucial. It gives us so many things – some of which we appreciate only when the work is not there any more. But see it in the perspective of life itself. If you take a prism and show it to the light, it will refract the seven colours of the rainbow. If we show the metaphorical prism to life itself, it will refract many different shades of life – work, leisure, love, friendships, pleasures, and so on.

Imagine life with only one metaphorical 'shade' – work. Sometimes we become stressed and anxious about our work, because we see life only in that particular shade. The more shades and colours you create, the greater the sense of perspective you are likely to have about life itself and where work fits into it. Hold the prism up to your own life and ask yourself what 'colours' are refracted.

Most of us experience this 'perspective' feeling most acutely when we go on holiday. We suddenly see a different world and are able to put work into perspective. But there are also people who seem to work purely for the annual two-week holiday in the sun. It is important, of course, to have things to look forward to, but not very useful if you have got back from holiday and have 11 months to wait for the next one. An answer may be to not see holidays in such a conventional form. Holidays can last a weekend or even just an

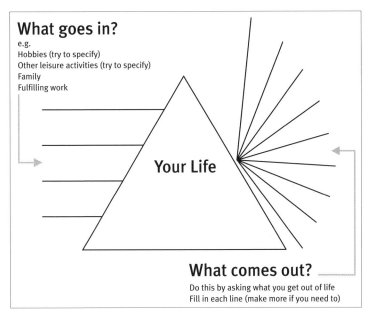

What goes in?
e.g.
Hobbies (try to specify)
Other leisure activities (try to specify)
Family
Fulfilling work

Your Life

What comes out?
Do this by asking what you get out of life
Fill in each line (make more if you need to)

evening. Variation in our lives is one of the things that places work in a truer perspective.

I recall one story of a man who saw his work as a dog and called it 'Rover'. Every evening he would put his working papers together in a pile, put them in a drawer, close the drawer and then head for his office door and shout 'Stay' in his loudest voice! This symbolic gesture allowed him mentally to sever the connection between his work and the rest of his evening.

So how balanced is your life? Find out by filling in the blank lines in the diagram above.

Accept there are many places you can work

Tough but true. The day after we leave an organization for a new job we are beginning to be forgotten. Within six months, most of your friends will be left behind – but you may have made a friend or two for life. Work is a fulfilling thing – absolutely central, I believe, to living – but it is also transitory. You have been valuable to your previous employer, but you will be equally or perhaps even more valuable to your next one.

A few of us will spend our whole life in one organization (this is more common in the public sector), but most of us will move a few times. Jacqueline uses an exit strategy to relieve tension. She knows she doesn't have to be there for the rest of her life, and knowing this (while running the risk of psychological detachment from your work) helps to keep the relationship between you and your employer a balanced one.

Remove negativity and negative people from your network

This is one of the tougher ones. We cannot always choose those whom we work with – you might well read this and say, 'My manager is my manager' or 'I cannot choose team colleagues.' This may be so, but we can choose the approach that gives us the best chance of establishing productive relationships. We look at assertiveness as a method for doing this later in the chapter (see page 136).

Challenge the rut you're in

If you want a challenge to the rut you perceive yourself to be living in, ask yourself, 'When was the last time I did something for the first time?' I recall a woman who had been on a stress workshop I ran returning the following year for a refresher course and coming up to me. She said she had started to ask herself that question every day, and had recently taken to hill and mountain climbing, which she had never done before. She told me that she had recently taken her husband with her to Mount Snowdon in Wales. On a particularly tough part of the climb, she turned to her husband and said those very words: 'Come on, when was the last time you did something for the first time?' This phrase has now become a permanent part of her vocabulary.

In the next section we assess the primary categories of workplace stress.

The four categories of workplace stress

Dr Karl Albrecht, in his book *Stress and the Workplace*, identified four categories of stress and anxiety at work. While one of these categories, 'anticipatory stress', is actually anxiety, the other three make us anxious about work only if we allow them to make us stressed. The four categories are:

Time: When there doesn't feel like there is enough time to do your work.

Anticipatory: Arising from the fear that something adverse is going to happen. This fear may be based on reality or otherwise.

Situation: When you are unclear about what it is you are trying to do and where you fit in, or there is conflict in the different roles you are trying to perform. Sometimes there is a feeling that you have no place to call your own in the organization you work for.

Encounter: Where we are uncomfortable dealing with certain people. These can be difficult people or they can be people with whom we have a very strong friendship. (An outside-of-work friendship can sometimes make it harder to ask someone a difficult question or request.)

We will now take each of these key areas in turn and offer some techniques that may help reduce anxiety in them. The critical factor in all of these categories is personal control. Even if we cannot dictate all the events that create difficulties in these four categories, we have the capability to control our reactions to them. Better still is the ability to take the proactive approach and this is particularly true of anticipatory anxiety.

(i) Time

Experts on the subject of anxiety and work-related stress, such as Professor Cary Cooper (whom I quote on the next page), believe that working more than 45 hours a week is detrimental to our health and well-being:

113

'If you work consistently long hours, over 45 a week every week, it will damage your health, physically and psychologically. In the UK we have the second-longest working hours in the developed world, just behind the States, and we now have longer hours than Japan.'

Many readers will identify with long-hours cultures and will recognize that, in the short term, we cannot do much about an employer who seems to demand it. It is naïve of any guide on workplace stress and anxiety to say, 'Start at nine, go home at five, take an hour for lunch, and have two 15-minute breaks, morning and afternoon.' It is naïve because we all know that doing this means, in all likelihood, being passed over for promotion, people talking about you behind your back and the best work being given to those who are seen to be more 'committed'. And, of course, having a pile of work to do and no time to do it builds up the anxiety inside us. The spiral continues as we start committing chunks of our evening to getting the work done. The sense of pleasure and relief from stress that we get from the idea of work-free evenings is killed by the impending sense of gloom as the home becomes an extension of the office.

As this is not a campaigning book, we need to look at the subject of managing time from a real, current world position. We start from the position you are now at in terms of your time and how you manage it, then, working back from that, try to see sensible working hours as something to which you can aspire as you regain control over the work you do.

EXERCISE

To start this process you first need to create a time log. For the next working week make a detailed log of what you do, the time you do it, and the time taken to do it. This will of course require a bit more of your time, but try to make the log as you go, rather than trying to remember everything you did at the end of the day. People who have done this report that, before they even begin to manage their time better (or in the words of Professor Cary Cooper 'work smarter' – see below), the log actually highlights a number of areas where they can instantly see time being wasted.

Now that you have this time log, you can begin the step-by-step process of clawing back the personal time being taken over by your job. Anyone who tells you that we are creating a revolution here is being unrealistic. But, by starting to include some of the personal effectiveness techniques in this 'Time' section in your working practices, the 'clawback' will begin to happen.

So how can I work smarter?

We have no choice about going to work but we do have a choice about the way we do it. Given that productivity is an indivisible element in workplace success, expert in workplace well-being Professor Cary Cooper suggests that what we need to do is not necessarily work 'harder' but work 'smarter'. It is a phrase that has been used for about a decade now without any discernable reduction in workplace anxieties and stresses, but many of us would agree with the sentiment. So how do we work 'smarter' and what does this really mean?

The tough part of this is that we know that the global success stories in the post-industrial economies of the last ten years, including the US and the UK, also have some of the longest working hours. The explosive growth of the Indian and Chinese economies, too, illustrates that economic success and hard work are not unconnected. The countries that have struggled economically, such as France, have shorter-work-hours cultures – indeed the 35-hour working week enshrined in French law is now widely seen as economic suicide. So what can we do about this apparent paradox? The answer may well be in thinking about the way we actually do that work. These answers, it has to be said, are not new. But even though we know how to work better, we often don't do it.

Many years ago I heard management guru John Adair speak at the press launch of a training video on managing your time at work. At the end of the film, a curious journalist said to him, 'Surely all this stuff is obvious? Surely it is just common sense?' To which John Adair replied, 'Common sense, yes. Common practice, no.'

Many people already know many of the basic principles of time-management. But how often do they keep to them? We know how important it is to prioritize first thing in the morning – a simple list of things to do ranked in the order in which they need to be done. That means prioritizing tasks for which the deadline is today. Some like to use a star system, as below; others employ a colour system.

* * * Three stars for those tasks that *must* be done or completed today, and which are important. Anything urgent is important.
* * Two stars for those tasks that it would be good to do today – perhaps because the deadline is tomorrow. Also for work that needs to be done on an ongoing basis for a future deadline – what we call 'progress tasks'. The work is moveable, but cannot be continually moved.
* One star for tasks where the deadline isn't immediate, but which, if the time were to become available, it would be useful to have completed.

This of course sounds simple. And it is. But the reality is, of course, that many things come along during our day to disrupt the well-planned routine. Because we know the day won't be perfect, some of us ask, 'Why bother planning for the perfect working day, when the perfect working day never happens?' The answer is that if we work from an already compromised position (the lack of planning), we compromise even further our ability to get the work done. If we start with best principles, we have a solid framework to work from, even if some parts of it have to be changed – in some cases, this could be more than once a day. In reality, many people find reasons not to manage their time, believing the uniqueness of their job prohibits it. But, in fact, no job benefits from a lack of planning and prioritizing.

Brian Tracy, in his book *Eat That Frog*, suggests that, having prioritized the day's tasks, we then tackle the toughest, least pleasant task right away (this is the 'frog' that has to be eaten). We are best at tackling the toughest tasks when we are at our freshest, and for most of us this means the morning. If we procrastinate and leave them until later in the day, we are tackling the difficult tasks when we are tired and thinking about the evening ahead.

So what about the day-to-day disruptions and interruptions?

Can you do this for me?

It is 4.30pm. Your day has gone well. You've checked off most things on your list of priorities. You need to get to get away at 5 today, and the two things that you have left to do will take you up to that time. Then your manager comes up to you and asks, 'Can you get this done by 5pm today?' What do you say? What do you do? Here are some options.

- Whenever anyone gives you a task to do, ask them how long they think it will take. If you disagree, ask if they are sure, and if you disagree, say so.
- Ask them what the deadline is. Most people, if they don't actually give a deadline, will say 'as soon as possible'. This isn't good enough for you. Ask: 'What is the real deadline?' You can then tell them if this will fit in with your schedule, or you can see if there is flexibility in your schedule. You can offer an alternative deadline if their deadline doesn't work for you.
- Don't just think, 'This person is my manager – I can't say no.' You don't need to. You can try putting the ball in the manager's court. Say to your manager, 'I have this and this to do by the end of the day. Which should I leave until tomorrow?' They might say, 'OK, I guess this could wait until tomorrow.' Or they might say, 'OK, I'll see if I can get … to do that job while you do this.' Remember, this isn't about being awkward in any way. It is, in a sense, a 'constructive no'.

Of course, there will be times when we will accommodate colleagues or managers, and so we should, particularly when there is a crisis on. But remember that we are very good at inventing unnecessary crises! Managing your time is not about being awkward, but it is about not being taken advantage of. Colleagues often take advantage of our accommodating natures, and managers are very good at coming regularly to the person who always says 'yes'. The problem is that the person who always says 'yes' is the one who doesn't get to leave work on time. Pretty soon, the work piles up and we begin to suffer the effects of overload. The idea of coming into work to tackle a never-ending pile of tasks – both ours and everybody else's – creates symptoms of anxiety. Being anxious about work often diminishes our capability to work at our most productive level. The downward spiral gets perpetuated and the anxiety increases.

Help! I'm drowning in paperwork!

Unfortunately, contrary to all initial predictions, computers and email have not led to a reduction in the amount of paper we handle. So we are left with an ever-growing pile of memos, reports, letters, sweet wrappers, magazines, marketing leaflets, and so on. If this is you, try to remember the (beautifully named) FART principle:

F File it
A Act on it
R Refer it
T Trash it

But don't keep looking at the same piece of paper over and over again, or returning it to the ever-expanding pile of paper whence it came. Try not to 'flit' from task to task, only half-doing each one. That little bit of extra effort to get the job done means you go home on time at night.

Meetings, and more meetings...

Advertising entrepreneur Winston Fletcher once said that 'meetings are places where great ideas are taken and quietly strangled'. All too often this is true, but, even worse, they also have a tendency to 'steal' vast chunks of the working day. How often have you sat in badly run meetings, for hours at a time, getting increasingly anxious about the pile of work back at your desk, and about the amount of your evening that that work is going to consume? Of course, plenty has been written on how to run meetings effectively, but here we are concentrating specifically on developing assertive behaviour to display within those meetings.

Perhaps the first thing to do when you are asked to attend a meeting is to ask, 'How long is it scheduled to take?' All meetings should have a start and an end time, and you asking the question will prompt the unskilled organizer to find out or to set the time limit personally. A reply such as 'It will last until lunchtime' isn't good enough. I like to eat my lunch at 12pm. You might like yours at 1.30pm.

The second is to identify clearly what your role is in the meeting. This is critical. How often have we attended two- or three-hour meetings when in reality we needed to be present for only 20–30 minutes? Take a look at the agenda in advance and, if you do not need to be there for the duration, state clearly what you see as being your involvement. Ask the organizer to call you when your bit comes up or, better still, ask at what time your part will be covered. You should, of course, make yourself easily contactable and available around the expected time of your participation. (Part of not wasting your time involves not wasting other people's. If your standards are high, those of others are more likely to rise to your level.)

The next step concerns your own preparation. Have the materials you need available and be clear about what your involvement is expected to be. If there are particular issues that you wish to bring up in relation to your topic, inform the meeting organizer so that they can inform others. Remember, others need to prepare too. If there is background reading to be done, make sure you do it.

Finally, do not attend meetings where no minutes are taken, or where minutes are taken but with no action points. In the same way that I cannot remember what I had for breakfast three days ago, I would not be able to remember much about a meeting held a week ago unless I had a written record to remind me.

The curse of email?

Let's go back 10 or 12 years to the time when email was just catching on. Remember how we were told how much time it would save us, and what an important communication tool it was going to be. In fact, through just a few years of misuse, it has become a frequent barrier to effective communication, and a classic 'buck-passing' tool.

Other people may make requests of us – difficult or otherwise – by email. Often, by transmitting a request in this way, the sender automatically assumes that the receiver has accepted the request. Of course, receiving an email is *not* the same as agreeing to its contents, but beware – others often try to imply that this is the case.

In a recent study by the Institute of Management/PPP Healthcare, email was identified as one of the top ten causes of workplace stress and anxiety. There are clearly some who recognize what a problem this has become. Organizations in the US and in Europe have instigated 'internal email-free days' and report that people actually start to talk to each other again; poor managers have nowhere to hide; and the buck-passers have to take some responsibility.

So how can you deal with email?

Instead of producing a routine list of 'Dos' and 'Don'ts', at this stage it might be useful to share the experience of someone with whom I once discussed this issue while on a stress-management course. We shall call her 'Cathy' from Milton Keynes. Some of the advice is risky, and I personally would not condone all of it (particularly on the use of the delete button), but I am sure many readers will relate to the circumstances. Some of the advice is very sound indeed although, in order for it to be successfully implemented, it requires an assertive approach (which we discuss later in this chapter).

STUDY

CASE

Cathy's story (Milton Keynes)

Cathy told me that she once came back from holiday to find nearly a thousand emails in her inbox. I asked her how she dealt with them all. 'I didn't,' came the reply. 'I just deleted the lot in one go. It was wonderfully liberating.' I asked if this caused problems for her afterwards and she went on to present her personal methods with little encouragement from me.

'No,' she replied. 'I found that if it was important people came back to me anyway. I may have missed the odd thing but can you imagine the feelings of stress and anxiety I had when confronted with this? I could have said goodbye to the next fortnight. If anyone caused trouble, I had a fallback position. I first asked them how they would go about responding to all these emails? And then I said I hadn't found theirs yet. These days what I do when I am away on holiday is to have a pre-prepared auto-reply: "I am away on holiday until… As I receive over 100 emails a day, I am unlikely to reach yours on my return. If it is important, please re-send it on the day of my return." I feel like I am playing a bit of a game, but I get a lot fewer emails now. I did get asked questions about my approach, but when I explained the situation most people admitted that they have the same problem. I think they admired my stance.

'I now make it absolutely clear to people that if it is important I expect them to tell me personally and not hide behind email. I like email – it does save time, but only when it is used as a proper time-saver.

'My approach did rub people up the wrong way. I am not denying that. I am quite comfortable saying what I think but I'll tell you what happened. After a while people responded to my personal methods. In the old days I could have spent two hours a day sifting through email. These days it is less than that, but I am happy with the amount of time I spend on it because I know that 90 per cent of it is relevant and important.'

A happy ending and an interesting approach from 'Cathy'. But it's an approach that does require us to be assertive in a way that generates a productive outcome. (For more on dealing with people using an assertive approach, see the 'Encounter' section on page 135.)

Others report some of the following techniques work for them:

• Try not to be a slave to email. Don't check your inbox every few seconds. Instead, try to put aside two or three segments during the day to work through your emails.

- Don't give up the precious first part of the day, when your brain is at its most fresh and active, to an administrative job like responding to emails. Just before lunch and before you go home are good times to do it.
- Make use of any email filter systems available to you.
- Be aware that the lifecycle of an email often grows exponentially once you send it. Are you merely wasting your, and others', time by doing so?
  And finally:
- If you are requesting good practice from others, be sure not to break your own rules!

Managing time within a team

If you work as part of a team, you could try some of the following techniques aimed at improving time-management. (Your colleagues may not agree with all your suggestions, but it's worth a try!)

- Arrange for each person to have an uninterrupted day each week to work on the stuff that needs real concentration and an uninterrupted passage of time. Studies show that to have anything more than 15 minutes of uninterrupted time in a day (what with phones ringing, colleagues asking you questions, and so on) is rare indeed, and under those conditions it's tough to produce quality work. It is bad policy to have total knowledge of one thing in one person's hands anyway – a sharing of knowledge and capability benefits everybody.
- Stagger lunch breaks. If it's always the same person left on their own to cover the phones while everyone else goes out to lunch at the same time, that person cannot hope to answer all the queries and questions in that time. It is simply adding to their personal stress – frustration at the lack of knowledge and inability to help being particular stressors. Callers are likely to be unsatisfied too.
- Ensure there's a good mix of jobs being passed around the team. If some people always seem to get all the difficult jobs,

while others get all the juicy ones, this can leave them feeling like they are being dumped on all the time.

• Try not always to turn to the same person – the one who gets the job done – in mini-crises. This places a serious burden on that person (it could be you) and, after a while, the risk is that that person feels 'burnt out'. Many enjoy the flattery of being the one who's turned to in a crisis, but the novelty soon wears off if our goodwill is abused.

Final point – people are generally reasonable if they are treated reasonably. When solving your own time challenges, be sure to treat colleagues with respect. This isn't about personal attack – it is about getting the job done and going home to enjoy some of the other things we want to get out of life.

How to do 24 hours' work in a morning!

Even with best 'smarter' working practices ringing in our ears, there will always be the odd morning that fills us with almost overwhelming anxiety. To cope with these times, there are some effective techniques that can be employed. It should be stated, however, that these techniques will work for you only occasionally – if you had to work like this every day, you would very quickly burn out! (If this scenario has in fact become the norm, you need to look seriously at your work, the way the work is managed and the environment in which you work. Is it right for you?)

Of course, in some jobs, such as working in the edit room the night before the next day's edition of a newspaper is being generated, we don't take the job on without understanding the lulls followed by the intense periods of pressure.

Edward De Bono suggests some good 'quick-thinking' techniques in his *De Bono's Thinking Course*. Here is one of them:

Five-minute problem-solving and decision-making: the TEC method

T – Target and task – 1 minute
E – Expand and explore – 2 minutes
C – Contract and conclude – 2 minutes

This is a great method for problem-solving or decision-making within a defined time limit. Imagine you have a problem to solve. The first stage, with one minute allowed, is to 'target and task'. In other words, define what the problem is and identify the question that needs to be answered. This stage is crucial – so often we attempt to solve 'the wrong problem' or poorly define the opportunity we see.

Stage two (two minutes) is to 'expand and explore'. In other words, to generate as many solutions to the problem as possible. Every idea gets written down. This is not the stage for criticism – it is about quantity, rather than quality, of ideas.

Stage three (two minutes) is to juggle the relative merits of the ideas generated in stage two and to decide which idea to run with. If the decision is being taken in a group, the whole group needs to commit to it.

In all three stages, the time discipline is sacrosanct.

When you need to work very quickly, the key question to ask is, 'What is the most important thing I need to do right now?' There is no slack in the day, so quick results are key.

Finally, do not forget that, when time is short, planning becomes even more important. The temptation, when faced with lack of time, is to remove the easiest thing to drop from our routine: a sure-fire route to failure, if ever there was one.

(ii) Anticipatory

All anxiety is in fact 'anticipatory'. Anticipatory stress or anxiety can work in two ways. We all have fears based on the possibility of events – whether real or imagined – occurring. In the first form of anticipatory anxiety we have such an expectation that 'bad things' will happen in a future scenario, that our attitude almost 'creates' the very circumstances for those bad things to happen. Later in this section we explore how this can occur when, for example, we have to make a presentation at work. These anxious feelings are natural, and probably have their basis in evolutionary processes. (Nearly all animals have some kind of instinctive fear – at its most basic level it is the fear of being eaten by another animal.)

In the second form of anticipatory anxiety, we foresee, with justification, the future event that makes us anxious. We respond in a number of different ways:

a. We do nothing.
b. The anxiety feeds on itself and we become even more anxious as a result.
c. We use 'anticipatory anxiety' as a positive emotion.

Let's look at these responses in more detail.

Doing nothing

Workplace anxiety can be debilitating, but this is often because we do not do the things we could do early enough to combat the anxiety we feel. We say to ourselves, 'If I hide, it will go away.' But often the circumstances that create that anxiety – difficult relationships at work, lack of time, and so on – do *not* go away. The danger is that, by doing nothing, we perpetuate and extend the circumstances that created that initial anxiety. Here is an imaginary example of how that might happen:

A failure to manage your time at work meant that you didn't get an important bit of work done, so you had to take it home over the weekend. You muddled through and got the work done, without addressing the real issue – why you didn't get the task done in working time in the first place. There may have been a very good, valid reason, but it may also have been because you wasted so much time during the day. You got the work done in the end, so the anxiety subsided.

A similar problem occurred a week later when you encountered a similar challenge. But this time the time pressure was a little greater. You believed that you would muddle through (because you did so before), but what you ended up doing was working late, taking the work home again, being irritable with your colleagues (thereby potentially damaging relationships) and increasing your anxiety about your lack of time. The next time… well, you know the rest.

The point here is that, if we do not take an honest look at the reasons why problems occur, by doing nothing we build in the possibilities for their recurrence.

The anxiety feeds on itself and we become even more anxious as a result

It is possible to be anxious about our anxiety. Imagine you have been told that a senior manager wants to see you tomorrow. A not unusual occurrence, and one that generates a not unusual response. You might, unless you already have a good, open, working relationship with that person, become anxious about the reasons for the meeting and ask yourself, 'Have I done something bad?' 'What mistakes have I made?' 'What is he/she going to ask me?' You might come up with some positive answers, but the negatives are likely to appear first, and in greater number. And, of course, negative thoughts increase anxiety levels.

In such a case you need to gain some control of the situation. If someone asks you for a meeting, ask what the meeting is for. Occasionally there may be very good reasons why you cannot know (for example, you are being offered promotion!), but in most circumstances the reasons are straightforward. If you need to justify your question, you can say, 'When I have a meeting I like to prepare.' By knowing the reasons beforehand, you are able to prepare yourself and make the meeting a more productive one.

In situations where you cannot know if the good ('You're getting a promotion!') or the bad ('We're going to have to let you go') is going to happen, remind yourself that these are once- or twice-in-a-lifetime events, and that your initial anxious response is not justified by their rare occurrence. Tell yourself that, where there is uncertainty, only personal control will allow you to respond positively to that uncertainty if it becomes real – even if the news is not as good as you hoped.

In the next section we look at making a pre-emptive strike through scenario planning.

Using 'anticipatory anxiety' as a positive emotion

The first signs of anxiety or, perhaps stronger still, real fear can provide us with the first essential building block in combating that danger we foresee. Feelings of worry, anxiety or even fear can be healthy if we choose a positive, optimistic approach to dealing with the cause of that concern. Indeed, this anxiety, if positively challenged, can help us to perform at a level we hadn't previously imagined.

So it is possible to learn to welcome feelings of anxiety, because they can provide us with an unexpectedly good opportunity to put a positive outlook on a situation. Let us pick an example of how we can do this and use it with Martin Seligman's 'ABCDE' model, which we introduced in an earlier chapter – you may find it useful to refer back to this model now (see page 63).

EXERCISE

Say you are one of the many people who do not like making presentations. For some of us at least that fear will have arisen from a bad experience. First, write down that experience (the '**adversity**') and the reasons why you felt the experience (the '**belief**') was a bad one. Or, if you have yet to make the presentation, write down why you believe it could or will go badly. The 'adversity' may have been that you got lost in your notes or the audience got fidgety and bored, for example. For 'belief', you might note down things like 'nervousness', 'fear of making a mistake', 'fear of no one wanting to listen', or 'I am not very good at making presentations anyway', and so on.

Under '**consequences**' write down what will happen to you if you feel the way you identified under 'belief'. For instance, you might try to avoid situations where you have to make a presentation in the future – a serious problem for the ambitious employee, where the ability to make a presentation is a critical workplace skill.

You can tackle the '**disputation**' issue in a number of ways. Take your beliefs and challenge them any way you can. Ask yourself:

- Is my reaction (the consequences) justified by the beliefs?
- Are those beliefs justified anyway? Remember: everyone comes to a presentation on your side!
- Why should I be spending so much time attached to my beliefs when they create negative feelings in me?
- Why do I have these beliefs anyway and are they true? As in life, the art of being successful or not in making a good

127

presentation will come down to how you approach it. (If you tell yourself that no one will want to listen you'll end up lowering your voice so that they will not have to hear you, with the result that no one will want to listen. Self-fulfilling prophecy delivered!)

- If you had a bad experience, what were the real reasons behind that? Did you create the conditions you feared yourself? Did you prepare properly? Was your fear of making a mistake rational? (After all, we all make mistakes.)
- What constructive actions can I take to avoid the 'adversity'?

Having challenged your beliefs, you should be able to see the possibilities of taking a different, more productive approach, and, as a result, the prospect of making the presentation '**energizes**' you rather than merely making you feel anxious. By working through this process, you have learned to be optimistic and to take the necessary actions to make success possible.

Being anxious about the big 'life changes'

We regard work as such a central focus of our lives that, when we see something coming that challenges the stability we derive from it, we can become anxious. A fear of redundancy, changes in the way we work, a new boss or rumours of a takeover or relocation are all examples of things that challenge that stability. In my books *Positive Thinking, Positive Action* and *Make Your Own Good Fortune* I suggest approaches we can take when these events are actually occurring.

When dealing with issues that can fundamentally affect our lives, it is important to recognize that our initial emotional reaction is entirely natural and normal. However, it's vital to bear in mind that this is also true in circumstances where we anticipate certain events taking place. In fact, the advantage of this situation – although we may be too anxious to notice it – is that we have the benefit of time to consider our options. Organizational 'grapevines' can be unhealthy when facts get converted into half or partial truths as the message filters through. But they can also provide us with an early-warning system – making us aware of something that could challenge our security. No matter how we hear this information (and it could be through our own intuition), we are likely to enter a process of emotional reaction (possibly including denial), reasoning why the anticipated event won't happen ('Why would they want to buy us?'), through to acceptance and finally to action as we decide what we are going to do about it.

Imagine a situation where you heard rumours of redundancy in your division or section. Your initial reaction would likely be an emotional one – 'disaster' ('It's because I am no good!'), possibly accompanied by denial ('It won't happen!'). You might then start to rationalize your denial ('The company couldn't survive without me/us!', 'The Manchester office is much more likely to be closed,' and so on). Only when you started to see the possibility of it happening for real might you accept its likelihood. At this point you might consider possible actions in response to this: anything from energetically looking for another job to going on strike.

Scenario-planning the big life changes

Think back to the imaginary situation in the last section – where you hear rumours of redundancy. Instead of settling for an emotional reaction, you can choose a more proactive approach to these changes. For example, you could opt to 'scenario-plan' – that is visualize a variety of future possibilities, both good and what may seem less good – and ask yourself, 'What would I do if X, Y or Z happened?' Keener observers might ask if we are not just sowing the seeds for greater levels of anticipatory anxiety by doing this. This will depend on our reaction to the possible scenario.

As we have seen, mild anxiety might actually be a good thing if it energizes us to have a constructive plan in our minds that can be applied if the visualized scenario comes about; we feel we have control because we have planned a response. However, where we blank the future scenario out of our minds, or just say, 'It will never happen,' then we deny ourselves the possibility of constructing a plan.

In reality, of course, we scenario-plan all the time, and the person who plans a positive response will be less anxious than the one who doesn't. This, naturally, is not an exercise to do all the time. But if we rest on our laurels we can find ourselves in for nasty surprises in a situation where our reaction may need to be almost immediate.

(iii) Situation

Lack of clarity about the role or roles we perform can be a source of workplace anxiety and stress. Some people don't care – drawing a salary is the sole point of going to work for them – but as the saying goes, 'If we go to work only for money, then money is the only thing we get.' However, most of us like to know what our role is because we measure our success or failure in that role by our ability to perform it successfully. But defining our role, as Karl Albrecht suggests, is a potential source of stress and anxiety.

Here are some typical anxieties relating to role, followed by some ways of overcoming the lack of clarity that causes them:

1. Where you are unclear about your role.
2. Where you are unclear about the freedom you have to perform in your role.
3. Where there is incompatibility between the roles you perform.
4. Where you are unsure about your own contribution.
5. Where you have conflicting demands placed on you, which makes it hard for you to be at your best in meeting those demands.
6. Where your role is undemanding.

Where you are unclear about your role

In this situation – where you are unclear what it is you are meant to be doing, and in particular what the priorities are – you need to seek clarity from more senior people, and in particular your manager. And, of course, when your manager delegates or empowers you to perform particular tasks, seek clarity on the priority of the task in relation to your overall work and the level of freedom you have to do it in the way you see fit. Most managers recognize that they are paid to get results through the people they manage, and will value the chance to discuss role priorities with you. If this is not the case, you need to make them aware of the dangers of not having clarity in this area.

Where you are unclear about the freedom you have to perform in your role

In the early 1990s, the breaking down of traditional hierarchical organizations was expanded to embrace 'personal empowerment', where employees were encouraged to display a greater level of self-determination in the way they approached their work. It was assumed that managers would have the ability to create the environment where people felt comfortable doing this.

In reality, you cannot leave your working future in the hands of a manager who simply doesn't have the psychological or emotional skills to create this kind of working environment. It is incumbent on you, therefore, to take responsibility and use initiative and proactive approaches. The inept manager is likely to be relieved that someone possesses that initiative (unless it threatens their power), and the good manager will be delighted that you are self-empowering.

Where you are unclear about your role and the freedom you have in it you should sit down with your manager and identify those parts of your job where you have freedom to do things your way and those things that have to be done in a very prescribed manner, or where you have to seek managerial approval first.

This approach will depend on the amenability of your manager. If they are not the most approachable of people, then you will have to make those decisions for yourself.

Where there is incompatibility between the roles you perform

We have many demands, constraints and choices in our work. We can find ourselves being pushed and pulled in different directions and often at the same time. Whom do we answer to?

Try thinking about your work in three areas:

1. The areas of your work where you have control.

2. The areas of your work where you have influence.
3. The areas of your work where you have no control.

Where there is incompatibility in the roles, it can help to assess into which group the work and the people affected fit. Where you have control there should not be an issue. Where you have influence you can use that influence either to encourage or discourage the affected person to see it your way or to have a change in policy. Or you can use it to play a more political game by reducing, over time, the importance or significance of the task. You may decide to perform the role anyway for political reasons, believing that your influence will help you to justify your actions if you need to, and that success will reflect well on you.

In the third grouping (where we have no control), we may decide, particularly where the other person concerned is senior to us, to do what is required, again for political reasons. Where there is a real incompatibility, we can try to bring the people together for resolution (the assertiveness skills we cover in the next section – 'Encounter' – will be important here), or we can explain our predicament to our manager.

Where you are unsure about your contribution

The need to feel that we are making some kind of contribution is essential to our own motivation – it gives us a sense of purpose. Traditionally, in larger organizations, it was harder to see how what we did fitted into the bigger picture because we were a small cog in a large machine. Being a small 'cog' made it easier to 'hide' if we were so inclined. These days, flatter organizations make 'hiding' far harder. Bad news for the lazy, but good news for the person who wants to be able to see more clearly where they have impact and where they make a contribution. That contribution is likely to be expressed through our relationships with others.

In the modern organization, our network of relationships is less likely to be 'top-down' (that is 'vertical') and more likely to be spread out through the organization we work for and beyond – like a spider's web. The following exercise will help you to assess the extent and magnitude of your own relationships at work.

EXERCISE

A useful exercise to help you realize how many people rely on your contribution is to draw a simple diagram like the one below. Place yourself in the middle and at each of the spokes write the name of different individuals, teams, departments, external suppliers, buyers, and so on, with whom you have working relationships. The list will soon be fairly extensive.

If you doubt the value of your contribution, think about the things that you do for all those people. Of course, the commitment we make to that contribution is another issue. But the more we value the contribution we make, the more committed we are likely to be.

A recent UK study suggested that 60 per cent of the working population believe that their work makes no contribution to society.

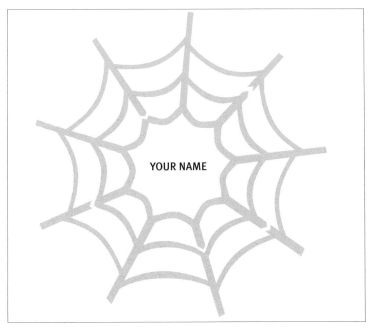

YOUR NAME

I did not notice if the survey said that the 60 per cent were worried about that, but its bias may be justified in that it recognized the need we feel to make a contribution. What we believe and what is real are often not the same thing. We do make a contribution – it is important to remind ourselves what that is. It protects us against a feeling of 'drift' and the anxiety-inducing vacuum that this can create.

Where you have conflicting demands placed on you

A classic example of this problem for the modern working woman or man is the conflict between the roles of parent and working person. In *Understanding Organizations* Charles Handy suggests (and many working parents in particular will recognize this) using the 'compartmentalization' approach so that roles do not overlap. He advises that, when you are at home with the children (fathers or mothers), you perform your role as a parent without keeping half an eye on your email inbox. And when you are at work, you shouldn't be making calls to the childminder or the nursery to check up on your children. No one pretends that this is easy, but the greater the temptation to self-administer ambiguity, the greater the possibility of you experiencing anxiety about performing well in either role.

To my way of thinking, at least, there should be no conflict in situations that are critical for your child's welfare and development.

Where your role is undemanding

In this situation there can be a temptation to be self-destructive, channelling our need to be occupied to negative ends. Proactive, positive strategies can have benefits – offering to take on more work, initiating projects, and so on. Where the role is undemanding, and you are satisfied that you are not misreading your role, you do not have an 'attitude problem', and you have tried a proactive approach, it is simply not helpful to continue in that role. 'Psychological retirement' can kick in at the age of 25–30, and I see plenty of 'one-company careerists' who are not there for any love of the job – only a stultifying weddedness to the comfort zone. You really must move on for your own good, or else retrain if your vocation no longer interests you.

The biggest role of all

Many of us don't know ourselves well enough at the age of 18–23 to make choices that could affect the rest of our lives. Quite often we 'land' in a job at the age of 20 or so – not through choice but because we need to start earning. Before we know it, we are 30 years old and recognizing that our vocation isn't a healthy fit for our likes, wants and interests. But we have worn the T-shirt for so long that, even though it is a bit moth-eaten and it doesn't fit as well as it did, we continue to wear it. In these circumstances, the 'psychological retirement' mentioned in the last paragraph kicks in very early and we are likely to idle the next 30 years away with little challenge and personal engagement. Does this induce anxiety? It certainly does if we feel that we want to be more than just making up the numbers. Some of us believe that work is inherently bad, and that there is no job that is right for us out there. And, like so many hard-headed beliefs, they will be true if you believe them to be so because your attitude will govern your actions. But many of us know that work *can* be good.

I meet so many people who reflect on how the 15 years from 30 to 45 slip by, and before you know it you have been in a monochrome working environment for 15–20 years. It is never too late to change, and modern society combined with a mixed economy makes this easier to do than it ever has been.

The same applies to younger readers who are slowly recognizing that work has not taken the hoped-for direction. Changing roles can be a big step, but never be afraid to look at what else is around. It could remind you that what you have is good (and sometimes we need to remind ourselves of this), or that something that is a better fit for us can be found elsewhere.

(iv) Encounter

We now come to the last category of Albrecht's sources of workplace anxiety and stress. This concerns the interactions we have with our work colleagues. Here the anxiety will usually arise when we anticipate a meeting or a verbal exchange with someone, or a group of people, which we think might be difficult or in some way uncomfortable.

It is often said that in human relationships 'we reap what we sow'. We covered relationships and how to generate stronger ones in the preceding chapter, and many of these skills will work for us equally well in the workplace. In some of the challenges at work that relate to people – dealing with difficult people, saying 'no', asking the tough question – it is our assertive approach that can help us make sure that:

- our rights are respected;
- we develop productive, professional relationships; and
- unacceptable demands are not placed on us.

We should not, however, underestimate the value of disagreement or conflict as an agent in getting improvements or clarity in the workplace. Where we focus on the issues, and keep personality away from it, disagreements can be productive. We can disagree without being disagreeable. But being assertive can also act as a preventative agent against future stress and anxiety – where we foresee difficulty, planning an assertive approach can divert us in a harmonious, positive direction.

EXERCISE

How to be assertive
In order to help this section relate to your own personal experience, try thinking back to times in the last 12 months when you have had to deal with a difficult person or a challenging situation, where the people involved may not have been difficult but the situation or the request was. Examples might include:

- Saying 'no' to a job that isn't yours or where you don't have the time to do it.
- Where you need to make a request of someone else and you know the person might not be easy to deal with.

Let us begin by defining what an assertive approach might be.

Definition

'Saying what we want, need, feel, think or believe in a direct, honest, appropriate and open manner that respects the rights of those we are addressing.'

Based on an original definition of assertiveness by Kate and Ken Back, assertiveness experts

There is often confusion about assertiveness and aggression. We say, 'He's very assertive,' when he is in fact aggressive because he is giving out orders, imposing his 'wants' on others and not doing a lot of listening. One of our rights is to be able to say what we think and to be listened to. This is a right often denied to us by those we say are 'assertive' when in fact they are imposing their will.

On the flip side of this, a sign of anxiety can be passive or 'non-assertive behaviour' – where we fail to say what we want, need, think, feel or believe, directly, honestly and openly. The reasons for this can be numerous – loss of confidence, low self-esteem, a poor relationship with the person concerned – or we are intimidated because the other person is our manager. It might be that we are someone who always says 'yes' to any request, or someone who shies away from contact with people we find difficult. Or it could be that we say, 'It was nothing really.' In passive behaviour we often diminish ourselves or fail to recognize successes.

Assertive behaviour will not always work for you, but it is the approach that gives you the best chance of a productive outcome. With people who are very difficult and with whom we cannot work – such as those identified in Jacqueline's story earlier – we can choose, where possible, to remove ourselves from their sphere of influence. And, of course, verbal or physical aggression is unacceptable and we have the right to walk away.

We can 'plan' an assertive approach if we are anticipating an encounter that may cause difficulty for us. In this next section we use a systematic approach to help us prepare for that challenge.

Situational visualization (SIV)

We begin with a general statement that we say to ourselves about the situation we are likely to find ourselves in, and about the approach that we should adopt with the other person whom we foresee causing us difficulty. Say, for example, you have to approach a colleague who has done a piece of work for you that wasn't up to scratch. You suspect that, while it was an important piece of work for you, it may not have been high priority for them and, as a consequence, it didn't get done properly. You might prepare the following SIV:

'This might not be easy, but if I keep in control of myself, and the situation, I will be OK. I know that they might not take this well but I must give them time to present their side of this too. I will listen, keep control, be positive and collaborative and try to resolve a positive agreed outcome. But I must also recognize that this is important and that my aim is to make sure that it doesn't happen again.'

Sound inner dialogue (SID)

If we are in a situation where we are anticipating an encounter with someone we perceive to be difficult, we need to prepare not only for the situation and the likely approach of the other person, but also for the range of possible responses. When we prepare a SID we have a conversation in our head about the upcoming exchange, which takes us through a variety of possible conversations. By preparing responses we leave ourselves better able to deal with the situation if it becomes real.

If we go back to the scenario we presented in the SIV above, we might anticipate that colleague responding in a number of ways:

- Complete disagreement.
- Presenting an excuse that doesn't justify the poor performance.
- Giving a very good reason that *does* justify it.
- Agreement with you.
- Embarrassment.
- Emotional reaction.

If your situation warrants it, you can create inner dialogues for all these possible scenarios. It must be said very clearly that in any situation where we need to be assertive with others we must maintain control of both ourselves and the situation. This isn't about being aggressive or bowing to the other person's wishes, but about maintaining a balanced perspective.

Having done a SIV and SID, we are then able to initiate an exchange. Timing and environment are important. If it is a sensitive matter, this should not be done in front of others and shouldn't be initiated when the other person is right in the middle of something else. But neither should a meeting be put off. In the chapter on relationships we look at some of the underpinning skills involved in building stronger relationships, and some of those skills apply here too.

When encountering someone who might be difficult, bear in mind the following simple checklist:

- **Remember what it is that you want.**
  Be clear what the purpose of you approaching that person is.

- **Find out if they see it the same way as you do.**
  The other person, like you, has the right to be heard. And they retain the right to disagree with you. Your style has to accommodate the views of the other person, so…

- **…Listen and ask questions.**
  True listening means putting yourself as far as possible into the other person's mind. Suspend your possibly prejudicial view of the situation. Ask open questions (who, what, why, where, when, how?) to check and confirm your understanding. A good sign that you are listening and asking questions is to see how much of the talking the other person is doing, particularly early on. They should be doing most of the talking at this stage.

- **Be direct (but not offensive) rather than circling the issue.**
  Tell them how you feel. Keep to the point. Allow pauses for thinking time, particularly if there is strong disagreement – it helps to control some of the emotional 'sting' in the situation.

- **Create a win-win situation.**
  Aim for mutual agreement and follow up on what you agree.

139

Remember – good relationships at work are about getting your work done. Sometimes you have to compromise close friendship for this, particularly when you have to make requests of those who you get on well with. But with a healthy, assertive approach to people, which respects their rights as well as yours, you can maintain good relationships and get the work done. People will respect you all the more for it.

The protective shell

In tough circumstances we need some sort of protective cover or 'shell' that moves us forward when the demands placed on us at work are starting to have an adverse effect. This adverse effect may take the form of a general anxious feeling about coming to work, or it may relate to something more specific. Whatever the circumstances, the adverse feeling we get means that at best (and it is not a good 'best') we cannot work to the level we are capable of and, at worst, if the feeling is left unchecked, our physical and mental health suffers.

A 'shell' provides us with protection and we can create our own shell through making a series of affirmative statements in our head about our ability to get through the challenges or when we find ourselves slipping into old bad habits. The art of thinking positively in situations at work that make us anxious is based around realism. Here are some examples of shell statements we can use:

- I will defend what I see as my best interests, but I understand that others have the right to do this too.
- I should be treated with respect and will respond appropriately when I believe I am not.
- I will assert what I believe are my rights, and will respect and honour the rights of others too.
- Difficult times mean I should be even more conscious of using the best practices I have committed to (managing time, for example).
- I will say, 'I don't know,' when I don't. But I will try to find out!

This personal 'shell' should not be seen as a vague series of worthy statements that we can sit back and admire. These are a set of governing principles, which must be translated into actual behaviour. You should work according to these statements and apply them in the situations that you find create anxiety for you.

A 'shell' can work for us in other walks of life too – in an earlier chapter we use it in connection with managing finance (see page 78).

Anxiety or stress?

This chapter has broadened the subject of anxiety to cover 'stress'. While anxiety outside the workplace has connotations that extend out into greater existentialist questions in the workplace, the two go hand in hand. Karl Albrecht identifies four causes of workplace stress, which have formed the backbone to this chapter, which are also the root causes of anxiety. If we fail to manage our time, work out our role, develop strong relationships or work with rather than against events that could affect our future, we can find ourselves naturally becoming stressed. But these stressed feelings will then lead directly on to an apprehension about our work and, at its extreme, a fear of even going to work in the first place.

As I suggested in the introduction to this book, all anxiety is based in a degree of apprehension about the future – even if that future is only a minute away. One of Albrecht's four causes of stress – anticipatory – is therefore at the root of anxiety. In this case the roles are reversed as the anxiety will cause the stress. But these are pedantic points. What is important to remember is that there are practical steps we can take to alleviate the causes. They will take time to master. The passive person will not immediately take to assertiveness and the aggressive person will find it difficult to button their lip, but with practice everyone can master these skills.

It also pays to remember that you are not tied to one job. If you define yourself purely by the job that you do, and you do not see yourself outside that role, it is not a healthy frame of mind to be in, because in troubled times your rigid thinking will not provide an exit strategy. As we saw in Jacqueline's story in this chapter and in Alan's and Heather's stories in earlier ones, having exit strategies (Jacqueline), retraining and/or changing your role in the organization (Alan), and changing jobs (Heather), can all provide a healthy way of seeing more dimensions to your life than the one that seems to be closing you in.

You are capable of doing so much more than one thing. Never forget that.

TIME:

'Whether you get off by being buried in the sand by a four-year-old or making a tour of French churches, you need to do something different every so often. Summer is a special time, I think, and should be relished. The blanket idea that all people should work more and have less time off for the good of their souls strikes me as peculiarly pointless.'

Mark Mardell, journalist, *BBC Website magazine*

Why don't we want to have fun?

At a recent children's party I attended, I was amazed at the anxiety created by the hostess as she ran the party according to a set of rigid and self-imposed deadlines. The first rule was that the party would last for two hours. She assigned a friend the task of keeping an eye on the time – 4.30pm being the pre-allotted time for the presentation of the cake – thereby passing her time anxiety on to somebody else. (This friend got anxious when, not owning a watch, she couldn't find her phone, which had the time on it.) At cake time, all the children, who had been having a fantastic time splashing around in the swimming pool, and who would have been happy to stay there for the next three hours, were suddenly whipped out of the pool. After cake, the children went to the back of the garden and played quietly on the grass – pretending

143

to do picnics for their dolls. But suddenly it was 5.30pm and, even though everyone had relaxed, it was time for the children to leave.

The unnecessarily rigid schedule imposed by the hostess meant that we all had nothing like the fun we could have had.

I saw this as a useful metaphor for the time pressures we put ourselves under. It is as though our concern for time has taken away the spontaneity that we need in our lives, and which acts as an excellent counterweight to anxiety. These captured moments of spontaneity are priceless. In this chapter we examine the benefits of taking your time and for allowing time for the things that are important to you. We identify five ways of rethinking your own notion about time and what you do with it.

(1) Rethink the past, present and future

We are continually exposed to major scare stories (some justified and some not) through the media and combating them does not mean sticking your head in the sand and hoping they will go away. Rather, we should revel in the fact that our race has survived, become infinitely more intelligent, innovative and resourceful, has provided amazing answers to some of the greatest problems confronting us, and shows no signs of being weaker than it has been at any point in the past. And there is no reason why this shouldn't continue in the future.

Recognizing what has happened in the past, what is happening in the present and what (good things) may happen in the future, can provide a valuable resource for those who are anxious about that future. In his book *Riding the Waves of Culture,* Fons Trompenaars suggests that all cultures of the world have slightly different time orientations. Some, such as those based strongly around religious beliefs, will see the present and the future only in terms of the religious teachings of the past. Cultures based very much in the present and the future, such as the USA, will be so because they have little past to refer to. Others, such as China, see a strong connection between all three – past, present and future. It is a subject that could provide hours of discussion but, for our purposes, we are concerned about the time orientation of individuals, because we too have them. Indeed, for many of us it is our cultural upbringing that has cemented our own particular time orientation.

So what does this mean as far as anxiety is concerned? The answer is that different orientations will have positive aspects, but also some dangers if we become too locked into living in one of them. As we look through past, present and future orientations you may find it helpful to give consideration to your own orientation.

Orientation towards the past

Positive aspects of this orientation

- We can learn from our mistakes – past mistakes provide future knowledge.
- Memories are important sources of joy and pleasure.
- Past achievements can build confidence for the future.
- History is mentally stimulating.

The dangers of being too locked in the past

- Feelings of melancholic 'wistfulness' take over as our thoughts concern an unrecreatable past.
- We become unable to relate to the world as it is.
- The belief that the past was great means that the present and the future are given no chance to succeed.
- We devote our energies to recreating the past rather than enjoying the present and creating a positive future.
- As our future gets shorter and our past gets longer there is a danger of feeling that there is nothing left to live for.
- We may fall prey to saying that the only path to take is the one that has always been taken.
- We run the danger of living our lives as an autobiography that has already been written and to which no further chapters will be added.

Orientation towards the present

> *'I try to make an active effort to achieve constant awareness of the daily beauty of life in all its small, intricate and trivial details.'*

> *Erica*, a colleague from Bosnia

Positive aspects of this orientation

- We allow plenty of spontaneity into our lives.
- We acknowledge and enjoy what is already around us – we live 'in the moment'.
- We deal with problems because we are more likely to see them as immediate.
- We adopt a 'just do it' attitude.

The dangers of being too locked in the present

- We can suffer from lack of motivation if we do not have things to look forward to or goals to be reached.
- Life can be directionless if we have no future-based thoughts.
- Lack of planning and forward thinking can mean nasty shocks.
- The lack of anxiety we may have because we live in the present can work against us. A controllable level of anxiety creates an early-warning system and a call to action.

Orientation towards the future
Positive aspects of this orientation

- We have goals to work towards.
- We tend to be optimistic or use our pessimism about the future to galvanize us into action.
- Our present efforts will be rewarded in future success.
- We will be motivated by the possibility of that future success.
- It reminds us that we are not immortal and creates action in us because we want to achieve things before our time's up.

The dangers of living in the future

- We never stop to enjoy the here and now.

- We run the risk of living in a fantasy world based in the future, but do little to make that world a reality.
- We ignore current challenges because all of our thoughts are dedicated to the future.
- Always thinking about the future can mean we become inflexible about what needs to be done in the present.
- If those big future goals are never reached, we may regret not having made the most of what is already around us.

A solution

There is a scenario that allows us extract the positive aspects of each of the time dimensions, and is summarized neatly in the diagram below. Three circles, each of which overlaps the other, represent the past, present and future time orientations. The idea is that we take the best bits of each of the circles (where the arrow is pointing in the diagram) and use these as a counterweight to the anxiety-inducing aspects of each of them.

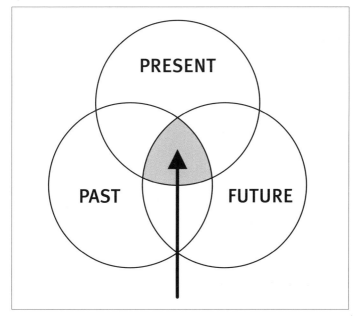

If we can develop a disposition that utilizes the three time dimensions:

- the knowledge and information that the past provides,
- the enjoyment and spontaneity of the present,
- a motivating and optimistic approach to the future,

we can add a wealth of positive approaches to deal with our apprehension.

I admit that there are many of us who are quite happy living in one particular time orientation, and I do not suggest for a moment that we should lose our connection with whichever one makes us comfortable. My point is that, if you are anxious, fearful or apprehensive, it might be because you are unwittingly locked into one of these dimensions, and need to look for a way out or an understanding of why you feel the way you do. To facilitate this, ask yourself the following questions: 'What have I done?', 'What am I doing now?' and 'Where do I want to get to?'

(2) Make decisions at the right time, not all the time

> *'Threat creates a mindset of anxiety and entrenchment in which awareness is constricted and focused on the avoidance of the threat, rather than the spacious, open attitude that the slow ways of knowing require to work.'*

Guy Claxton, *Hare Brain, Tortoise Mind*

We often create a kind of false pressure for ourselves by imagining that we don't have nearly as much time as we do. For example, when making decisions, we often feel pressurized to do so too quickly. This isn't about procrastination – it's about when we *need* to make those decisions. Guy Claxton, whose quote opens this section, talks about how the brain 'thinks' even when it is not consciously doing so. And a combination of different thinking processes in our unconscious, subconscious and conscious minds will often generate solutions we may not have considered had we been pressurizing ourselves for answers.

Think about a time when an idea jumped into your head while you were chewing over a subject slowly rather than 'hard-thinking' a solution. These 'eureka thoughts' often come about as a result of the slow thinking that takes place in our unconscious mind, and which makes a connection with our conscious thoughts because we are giving it time to do so. Would you have arrived at a solution if you had significantly reduced the time available to you to come up with an answer? Probably not. We perhaps say to ourselves that, because of the time pressures we choose to attach to our own lives, we need to rush a decision so that we can free up brain space to consider the possible solutions to the next one.

But, in reality, all we may be doing is coming up with the best solution given the limited amount of information we have picked up in the limited amount of time we have allowed ourselves. So for those with time anxieties there is value in asking:

- How much time do I really have to make this decision?
- Once I have given the problem or opportunity a place to lodge in my mind, can I then stop myself from 'overthinking' and attempting to force myself to come up with a solution?
- Can I back myself to arrive at a solution when I am not apparently thinking about what that solution might be? (This is about being prepared to trust both our intuition – which may take time to work – and deeper thought processes, which will be working towards solutions even though we may not be conscious of thinking about them. In this situation we apply a kind of mental 'dimmer switch'. The light is still on, but dimmed so that it is barely shedding light at all. But it is still working.)

As Guy Claxton's quote suggests, threat and fear can leave us prone to anxiety, which forces us to make quick decisions to help deal with the threat or fear. We often have far more time than we imagine. Don't be afraid to make use of it.

(3) Create 'margin'

Richard Swenson has written extensively about what he calls the 'margin' in people's lives – the space we leave for rest, relaxation, leisure and sometimes just for contemplation. Many of us seem to have very little 'me' time, and surveys show we are also getting less sleep than we used to. It seems that watching the TV is filling much of this extra time. In spite of what is said about the 'long hours' cultures in post-industrial societies, the majority of us have more leisure time and work fewer hours per year than at any point in the last 500 years. We have a minimum of 30 weekdays off per year (bank holidays plus legal holiday entitlement) as well as an additional 100–120 days off (weekends/weekdays) depending on the nature of our work week. And yet we say we have less time than ever before.

There is considerable evidence to suggest that the majority of this extra time may be spent in front of a TV or computer screen. The issue may not be so much about time as about what we do with that time. Are traditional relationships and bonds (family, community, and so on) suffering because of the fragmented nature of our free time?

Try leaving the 'margin' blank

The ever-expanding universe comprises billions of stars, planets, antimatter, dark matter, black holes, and so on. In other words lots of 'stuff'. But, between the 'stuff', huge amounts of space contain almost nothing at all. The universe works as much because of this empty space as because of the 'stuff'. We have lots of 'stuff' in our own lives too. But, like the universe, we probably work better when we are prepared to entertain the idea of open space, and are happy not to have to fill in the gaps. Great scientists and writers report that they were often content to spend half a day just 'thinking'.

To learn to do nothing, to contemplate, or perhaps to meditate, but to learn not to have to be doing things continuously, is a skill that takes a long time to master. But, if you can learn to do it, it can help return balance and order to your life.

In a different form, the famed Mediterranean siesta is a way of resting when energy levels are low anyway – in the hot mid-afternoon. Most people, I'm sure, think that this is a very, very good idea.

So the lesson is, where you can, not to feel guilty about doing nothing. Your thoughts can be random and take you where you like. The most important thing, however, is to forget about time.

Take time out for breathing

A simple technique to help you achieve a more peaceful, less anxious state – and I am told one that works well with people who have trouble going to sleep – is to practise the 7/11 breathing technique.

EXERCISE

Simply breathe in for a full seven seconds until your lungs are full. Then spend 11 seconds breathing out until your lungs have fully exhaled all the air (mostly toxic carbon dioxide). Keep doing this for a couple of minutes. Once you have created a good rhythm, close your eyes (if you haven't already) and carry on breathing rhythmically. You can then, if you wish, and only after your breathing pattern has become regular, feed into your thoughts things that give, and have given, you pleasure. You will take yourself to a happy place. But you can do this equally well without filling your head with thoughts.

I recall doing a ten-minute version of this exercise with a group of people one sunny afternoon in a classroom in a hospice. Two of the group were asleep almost instantaneously, and one of them slept on for around 20 minutes. He reported feeling very refreshed afterwards, once he had got his bearings!

Rhythmic breathing is actually very important in other ways too. When we are anxious we need a good regular supply of oxygen to the brain to keep it working at its best and able to think clearly when we most need it to. But we all know that one of the first things that goes when we are under pressure is the ability to breathe properly – breathing in and out in a settled and consistent manner. Highly anxious people tend to 'gulp' air. Those who are less anxious probably breathe a little more quickly, but don't allow themselves the time to expel all the air from their lungs that they should. People in full panic mode may even start to worry about their consistent breathing, worry about it more and make their breathing even worse.

In the preceding chapter, and in particular in the section on dealing with personally challenging situations, we looked at 'sound inner dialogue' and 'situational visualization' as methods for preparing ourselves for an upcoming challenge. The 7/11 breathing technique is another useful technique for this. Try to imagine yourself successfully dealing with the thing that has caused you anxiety in the first place – but don't feed this into your thoughts until you have been breathing rhythmically for a few minutes. It is important to get yourself into a relaxed state first.

This process of visualizing yourself being happy or successfully coping with problems, while in a relaxed state, will enable you potentially to deal better with anxiety-causing future scenarios.

In order for this technique to be successful, you do need to create the 'margin' we mentioned earlier. How might you go about this? I use the four historic natural elements, air, earth, water and fire, to illustrate.

(i) Element air: Enjoy just being at home
The first thing is to change the way you actually view your domestic surroundings. When we go on holiday we frequently try to get as far away from domestic surroundings as our budget will allow – often abroad. By doing this we run the risk of associating our local environment, including our home and the town we live in, with a place where we cannot relax. We act as though the metaphorical 'breath of fresh air' exists only in a far-away place. But we can learn to 'freshen up' in our local surroundings, and not treat them as though they were 'polluted', or as places full of stressful baggage where it is impossible to relax.

If the only place we can freshen up our lives is over a thousand miles away, we resign ourselves to just four weeks of true relaxation per year (if we can afford it). Can you slow down enough to enjoy what's around you?

(ii) Element earth: Take time out
This takes us back to the things we enjoy the most – those that are a natural part of us and that help us to relax. Element earth is about

nature and the pleasure we can derive from it. In our pressurized state we often fail to find time to access the things we enjoy doing the most. In this exercise we try to re-energize ourselves by stimulating the five senses: taste, touch, smell, sight and hearing. The exercise is simply to 'state and date' – that is, to state which of the senses we want to stimulate and when we can build doing this into our lives. (This may seem a little contradictory, I know, when I have said that we are trying to move away from time considerations, but in the early stages we do need to plan to build in these natural stimulants until they become part of our natural rhythm of life again.)

Here are some suggestions as to how we can stimulate the senses:

Taste: Cooking a great meal and taking time to eat it rather than racing to get to the telly, kissing someone you love.
Touch: Your partner's body, the soil, your children, fabrics, wood, food.
Smell: The pages of a new book, the seaside, the country, food, smells that bring back memories.
Sight: Architecture, old friends, something new, looking up in the city rather than straight ahead.
Hearing: True silence, live music, the birds.

Failing to stimulate the senses is not good for our mental well-being. We quickly move into a state of what I call 'none-sense' – running around at a pace dictated by everyone else and never slowing down to enjoy what's around us. The lack of pleasurable and healthy stimulations denies us an outlet for the stresses and strains of modern living. Giving ourselves time to release the pressure by doing something else takes our mind away from current anxieties. And we find that the time away helps us to be more relaxed and therefore better prepared mentally to deal with those anxieties on our return.

(iii) Element water: Getting clarity

With our packed time-stressed lives, it can be a great help to lose some of the physical and psychological clutter that we seem to accumulate.

Getting clarity – the purity of nice clean water – frees up time and freshens up our mind.

I took once a three-week break from my work and the irony was that after the break I noticed how much progress I made in my work – even when I wasn't actually doing it. I was happy and relaxed and came back fresh and was much more productive. People cannot be like this while they are working all the time. I use a simple story to illustrate the point. It is one many of us will have experienced, if only once or twice in our lives.

CASE STUDY

Arlind's story (Pristina, Kosovo)

The value of taking a break was bought home to me a couple of years ago when I went to a village with some friends of mine. We visited an elderly couple who were very content with their life.

This couple had an old house with a beautiful garden where, not surprisingly, they spent most of their time. They had a simple life, but it seemed to us a very full and 'occupied' one even though they weren't always doing things. They seemed to know when to slow down.

They did not have a TV, just an old radio which played music most of the time. My friends and I spent three nights in their house, and those nights I will always remember. During the day we learned various things about nature and enjoyed the views and the fresh air. You can only imagine what a bunch of city boys felt like in such a relaxing environment. During the evening we spent the time sitting out in the garden, looking at the sky, sharing our thoughts and experiences together. Even though there was no luxury, I don't remember looking at a clock at all!

Perhaps our hosts were anxiety-free and happy because they didn't have any great expectations from life other than the enjoyment of natural things. We of course had a different range of experiences and our expectations were different. Those three days away completely

*revitalized me. I had shut my mind off from other things and came
back refreshed and full of energy. For a while, at least, I learned
not to get stressed about things that actually don't really matter.
That fact that I still remember it really well tells you how such
a simple experience stuck in my mind.*

(iv) Element fire: Time to get the old energy back

We are all born with different amounts of energy. Some of us seem
to thrive on a life of action. Others seem happy to live almost like a
contentedly dozing cat. But few of us would deny that, particularly
as we reach the age of 30–35, we would like to have more energy.
Feeling anxious? Making time for energy-creating pursuits makes us
feel better and alleviates the symptoms of anxiety. Here are some
suggestions for the kind of things we can do that help generate energy
and renew enthusiasm:

- Exercise builds up your physical and mental resilience. It
  purges the brain and body of the flotsam that slows them down.
- Inject variety into your life. Take different routes into work;
  meet your family after work at somewhere other than your
  home; turn off the telly and do something else; learn to play a
  musical instrument.
- Anxiety shuts down the personal fun factory almost before
  anything else. In anxious times we have to work hard to
  re-inject that fun and energy. Don't cut out the very things that
  can help you get out of your current situation.
- Energy-inducing pursuits are self-perpetuating. New energy
  creates more of the same.

(4) Make haste slowly

There is often some value in questioning the things we do and, in
particular, the way we choose to do those things. In this next case study
we hear from Marco, a London-based van driver who carved up the

road, boy racer-style, until he saw the stupidity, in his case, of what he was doing. It all comes down to learning to slow down a bit...

Marco's story: *A courier's tale*

I work as a van driver in London. I am, or rather I was, the archetypal 'white van man'. Tearing round narrow streets, not stopping at crossings for pedestrians, cutting other cars up – you know the type.

Every day I would pick up or deliver around 30 items. I remember on the way in to work I used to get anxious about the day ahead – thinking about the abuse I would no doubt be throwing at other drivers and they at me, working out how to get from one side of London to the other in 20 minutes (not possible – I tried!), and so on. I even drove like a madman to get to work.

One day I found myself having to do a delivery on Saturday. As I was looking after my young daughter that day I had her in the van with me. I had only one delivery to do and I had all morning to do it. But I still drove at a ridiculous speed as though that were the only way I could drive. I drove right into the back of a BMW and wrote it off. My daughter was absolutely fine, but the crash terrified the life out of me. What if she hadn't been OK? What if it had been someone else's daughter? You think things like this will never happen to you but, you know, they do. All because we can't slow down a bit.

Someone described the state I get in now as I drive as 'zen-like'. I watch other drivers treating the road like a racetrack, and find myself laughing at them. If I get stuck in a jam, I just live with it. I can't do anything about it, so why get uptight? I now take the attitude that 'what doesn't get done, doesn't get done'. But you know what? It always does. And what I have found is that my day probably takes only ten minutes longer than it did before when I was driving like a lunatic. And that seems like a small price to pay to preserve my mental health and the physical health of others.

I always remember a study that said a person who drives 200 miles from Manchester to London at 90mph will arrive in London only 5–10 minutes ahead of the car that does 70mph on average. I never believed it before, but I do now. Why are we all in such a hurry?

Time is a relatively new phenomenon. Its importance really came into play in industrialized economies only at the beginning of the 19th century, when we developed a more structured approach to work. We quickly moved from a position where the greater part of the population was self-employed to one where employers needed to organize this work. Time became all-important. In addition, life expectancy was not high, so many of us were concerned about living in, and enjoying, the present.

However, as Marco's story helps to illustrate, time has become a controlling beast. It's an old saying that goes, 'Slow down or nothing worthwhile will ever catch up with you.' But faced with a bombardment of messages telling us that the stakes have never been higher, we think we have to 'run' continuously to keep ahead of the 'game', or break into a full sprint to 'win' rather than just get across the finish line. But, of course, this is a race that actually doesn't have a finish line.

So some of the key lessons here are:

- If you feel that you do not have enough time, think about how much time you waste.
- Do not feel guilty about taking a break. There is nothing heroic about heart disease caused by overwork.
- Laugh at the person who indulges in non-productive manic activity – don't try to copy them.
- We all operate at different speeds. Choose the one that is right for you, not the one that someone else decides is right for you.
- As we saw earlier in the chapter, it is perfectly all right to do nothing sometimes.

157

• Make time for what is important. Your family and friends need you. And you need them.

(5) Enjoy guilt-free time out

One hundred years ago we used the amount of leisure time available to us as a measure of 'success'. The more leisure time we had, the less we were working. And if we weren't working it was because we didn't need to. Most of us had a life of unremitting labour – generally hard labour. A half-day on a Saturday and the reluctantly granted Easter holiday was as far as it got for some. In the US, at the time when Stevie Wonder and others fought for Martin Luther King Day, the arguments against the idea were often about 'another day off' rather than about the chance to celebrate the life of Dr King.

In the UK, the argument against adding a bank holiday between August and Christmas was that 'industry needs a good run in the three months up to Christmas'. If 90 days isn't enough, would the 91st make all the difference? But would the workforce and their productivity benefit from an extra day off to catch their breath? More than likely. Nowadays we can be made to feel guilty for having a bit of time on our hands. Time, for some, has become a space that has to be immediately filled, and prosperity seems to come packaged with high levels of stress.

Of course, it is perfectly possible to work hard, be prosperous and still have a sense of perspective about what is important and what isn't, and when to stop. And it begins with cutting out the ridiculous idea that taking 'time out' is wasted time. Or that we should feel guilty about getting a bit of 'me' time. Recognize that we have as much or more time than we ever did. But we have less 'free' time because we are becoming obsessed with filling every waking moment. This is, of course, a version of that old maxim that says, 'Work expands to fill the time available.' Like Marco the driver, we have become very good at creating manic activity where none needs to exist.

Conclusion – It's easy to judge

Imagine you are 16 years old, and have been bought up on one of London's poorer estates. The local 'success story' is a young man, six years older than you, who drives a top-of-the-range Mercedes, is well dressed, has a coterie of admirers and deals in crack cocaine. You, of course, have a choice here. You might believe that, given those circumstances, the career path is obvious. By emulating this man, you could earn in one year what it might take 30 years to earn in the mainstream. Or you might take the conventional path – but, given the job choice available, that might mean doing something unglamorous and menial.

It is of course easy to make a series of moral judgements here about education, lack of morality and parental influence with a whole load of prejudice tacked on. What might you be like if you had been born into this situation? Although this is an extreme example (and one where the behaviour is illegal), it does, I feel, illustrate a point. Many of us are impatient for success, and will create any short circuit we can in order to obtain it. When we have success we want to flaunt it. But the success is vacuous. I might be naïve, but I believe that if we work towards something, do our best, are patient and choose a vocation that fits with the type of person we are, we will be much happier, on reflection, as a result.

Be patient. Particularly if you want to be around to enjoy the successes you will have.

THE FUTURE:

What does it hold?

'Staying alive is a lot less fun than being alive.'

Source unknown

Not being happy can cause anxiety. But being happy doesn't mean you have eradicated anxiety. In fact, some of us, as we try to overcome our anxiety through our own positive actions, may well revel in the fact that this anxiety pushes us to take on new challenges that provide the fulfilment we seek. In addition, part of the accessing of happiness, particularly for mature readers, may well come from conquering many of the anxiety-inducing challenges that life throws at us.

So if I were to ask you now, 'Are you happy?', how would you respond? Perhaps more important than the question itself are the criteria you use to try to answer it. Some people will respond by compartmentalizing their lives – work, family, fulfilled leisure time, and so on – to try to build an overall picture. Others will immediately reply that they aren't happy, pinpointing one or two reasons because these things are constantly on their mind. Most of us, however, are likely to ponder the question for a while as we weigh up the pros and cons in our own lives. Perhaps, as someone once said, when we are truly happy we don't realize we are. When we have to ask the question of ourselves, we probably aren't.

This, the final chapter in the book, concerns your future. Many writers agree that we have many more anxieties than we used to, and many studies indicate that we are less happy then we were, say,

161

DON'T WORRY: How to Beat the Seven Anxieties of Life

50 years ago. And this at a time when life should be so much easier than it was then. So what can make us happier and less angst-ridden? There are no definitive answers, only informed suggestions, and in this final chapter we give some pointers as to how our lives can be happier if we are prepared to make a long-term commitment to that happiness.

We begin by referring again to the responses I received to the 'happiness questionnaire' I sent out before beginning to write this book, and which we also looked at on page 81. I make no comment on whether I agree or disagree with each statement – in fact I would not want to. What delights me is that each respondent has a clear idea about what it is that makes them happy, and what it is that seems to make others they observe happy. This was a small study, but the comments, I would imagine, are not unusual and I hope, to some readers at least, will be helpful.

Moving to new countries, whether for work or study, has always increased my happiness by exposing me to new and interesting people, situations, and opportunities to experience life.

Erica, Bosnia

I have to be in control of my own destiny as much as possible. The more in control, the happier I am. (I should add that I do not have to be in control of others!)

Neil, UK

Let me try to be deep now. Happiness is a state of mind and, when tied to life, it is like a rollercoaster ride. There are highs and lows at any point in anyone's life (unless they live in Utopia). To put this in context, while in Europe, I observed friends who were kind of happy that the weather was beautiful so they could go to the park to have BBQs or to a beer garden, or that they were able to afford a holiday to some sun-drenched beach.

162

When I visit relatives back in Kenya, I have observed real happiness in parents whose kids are able to get basic education, parents who are able to put food on the table on a daily basis, parents who are able to buy a new set of clothes for their kids at Christmas... Bottom line: parents who are able to afford the basics to make a comfortable family life are very happy.

William, Kenya

Life's too short to be miserable, and whatever situation one might be in, we, as individuals, should look at people around the world who are less fortunate than us, and give our thanks and not be ungrateful.

Ismail, UK

Respecting one another in all aspects of your life can create a positive reaction, which makes not only yourself but also others around you seem happier.

Wendy, USA

Striving for what I feel is right and just, believing in myself and trying to create a happy environment for those I love – these components makes me happier. Also, I am happier in realizing that no situation is perfect, and that I am lucky to have the things that I value and treasure.

Lorna, UK

Taking positive steps to shape my life when possible.

Debbie, UK

I certainly feel happier when I feel healthy and totally believe there is a direct causal relationship between the two. So, if I eat well, exercise, get good sleep, drink less and generally look after myself, then usually I feel significantly happier than when I do the opposite.

However, the idea of 'taking action' to make me happier is a stranger to me. Whether it's because I wallow in being miserable or indeed because I feel incapable of taking such action, I seldom look to rectify a situation that is making me unhappy.

Carlos, UK

People are happy when loving each other, when loving animals, when appreciating nature, when doing what they like (sports, reading, a job they like/can do, shopping, talking, travelling), when they have things to believe and dreams to cultivate (typical of youth).

Daniela, Italy

Our society is geared towards the 'me', which is often very nice to escape from. Looking at families and lasting marriages makes me happy, as does the beauty inherent within children. Their unscathed innocence makes, I think, most people overjoyed at the beauty of God's creation.

Nina, UK

The people who do not expect too much from their life; who always are ready to help others; they are the happiest people.

Lionel, Sri Lanka

To be healthier, wealthier, more focused and to worry less! To do more exercise that I enjoy doing when I want to do it – not just gym punishment early in the morning or late at night; to have paid my mortgage off to a manageable size – half what it is now; to get clarity on what I am going to focus on this year; to concentrate on those things I can do something about and to stop worrying – easier said than done!

Susan, UK

From reading these quotes, it would seem that many of us have a very clear idea about what it is that makes us happy. Equally compelling is how few mention money, possessions and stratospheric achievement as the means to that end. So we have a paradox where the very things that society now seems to suggest are the badges of status and success are really not the things that people believe will make them happy. I do not think there are definitive answers to this question, but I do believe that there are certain factors that can, over time, help us to recognize and access that which can make us happy. They do not work for all the people all the time, but at least some of them provide a helpful direction when it is needed. I believe that by recognizing these factors we remove a number of unnecessary anxieties from our lives – or at least learn not to take them so seriously.

(1) Beyond base camp

There is no question that we need to consume and possess at a fundamental level. The absence of the essentials for living, such as food, water and adequate shelter, implies a brutalizing existence that is beyond the scope of this book. What we in post-industrial economies define as 'basic' will be different depending on our environment. Of course, with each generation, what constitutes the 'basics' changes. What is important is not what you have and possess over and above the necessities but the value that you place on having it.

The basics get us to the happiness 'base camp'. Once we have them looked after, for most of us anything that we add probably doesn't significantly add to our happiness. Other factors come into play, about which I hope this book has provided some guidance. Try to consider whether some of your anxiety comes from a misunderstanding about what might make you happy.

(2) The highs and lows are part of life

Many of the respondents to the 'happiness questionnaire' referred to the ups and downs of life – 'no situation is perfect', 'life is a rollercoaster ride' – acknowledging that part of the fabric of living is

165

to be realistic about what can happen. This is not something to be depressed about – it is something to be honest about.

Of course, it is naïve to expect that, just because some book tells you to 'recognize that the highs and lows are part of living', you will now go away and believe it. This viewpoint may develop over time and through your own experiences. But I believe that those who carry this belief with them, even if it isn't deeply held at the beginning, are more likely to embrace the highs and lows as they go through life. It is a great sadness to me when I come across those in their 60s or 70s who haven't grasped the idea that the highs and lows are part of life's experience, and not a bad hand of cards that have been dealt to them throughout their life. I believe that, as the cards are dealt, at least some of them are 'face up'. We can choose to play them or ignore them.

Your happiness will come from the way you relate to all of your experiences – good, bad and indifferent.

(3) Big government

Historically, governments existed to create social cohesion and prevent anarchy and perpetual war between local factions (and, if I am being cynical, to protect the interests of the ruling classes). This was abused for centuries – the rallying call to create social cohesion and togetherness was often war against neighbouring countries or different sub-cultures (religious groups, for example). After the two great world wars of the 20th century, people had had enough of fighting and governments decided that their role was to make people happy – it was believed that happiness came through the provision of good healthcare, education, local facilities, and so on.

But, and it is a big but, if we believe (as studies seem to indicate) that people are less happy and more anxious now than, say, 50 years ago, we can conclude that governments have been spectacularly unsuccessful in their attempts. Governments now generate indices where they identify the best places to live in their country and use the 'schools and pools' (education and leisure facilities) criteria to do this. I wonder, however, if the people who live in these places feel any happier than those who don't.

It seems to me that, when it comes to trying to improve our world, making ourselves happier or less anxious, or indeed enhancing our life in any other way, the only thing we can be certain of is ourselves. If you want to be happier, it is likely to be *you* who will make that happen. If you want to be less anxious, it is going to be *your* actions that reduce your anxiety. If you want a better life, it is *you* who will generate the conditions for that.

Now, it may be that great things will happen over which you have little control – the joy that your parents feel when they become grandparents adds immeasurably to their lives, for example. But you cannot rely on events over which you have little or no control happening to make you happier.

It is your life and what you do with it will make the difference. If you are happy to 'be', just 'be'. If you want to be something, try to 'be something'. If you want to be something special, try to 'be something special'. But know yourself well enough not to try to be something or someone you are not.

(4) Who sets the agenda?

Worrying about what others think lets us fall prey to what De Botton calls 'the weak capacity for independent judgement with an appetite for the views of influential people'. In other words you are judging yourself and your suitability for status on the values of those who are not qualified to make judgements about you and your life. So do not let them. Your agenda for living should be set by you, not by somebody else.

(5) The good news – as well as the bad

If you are prone to anxiety about global issues, try to find balance. If the 20th century was the century of ideology, in the 21st we may be dancing to a very different tune. In the very week I am writing this, there are two recurring themes on the news as I turn the radio on in the morning. The first concerns the decreasing amount of fresh water available to us through the lack of rain, and the second is the price of oil. It seems that we may have too much water (because of the melting ice caps) and not enough water (because of global warming) in different parts of the world. As far as oil is concerned, we know this is a dwindling resource. This may well be the century of the scarcity of these and other resources. Are you anxious about this? I am. We have every right to be.

But one less publicized media report from the same week contained some very good news about the environment. The hole in the ozone layer above Antarctica has stopped growing because of the ban on CFCs. Blink and you would have missed the story because we have become so obsessed with the negatives. We have every reason to believe in the capacity of humans to survive and thrive as we have done over tens of thousands of years through our own affirmative actions. Indeed, you may be one of the people whose anxiety about the future makes you become actively involved in making it better for all of us. Great! And a good example of the positive, galvanizing effect anxiety can have.

CONCLUSION

This conclusion is divided into two parts. In the first section I suggest four positive statements that, if you apply them to your life and the way you are currently living it, will help you to carry forward and implement many of the messages from this book.

In the second part I list ten quick ways to reduce anxiety and increase positivity in your thinking and actions. You could regard it as a 'bonsai' version of the whole book.

Part One – The four statements

Positive statement 1

I will make an effort to distinguish between 'having to' and 'wanting to'.

We have seen throughout this book that, even when huge restrictions are placed on our personal freedom, we always have the refuge of choosing our own attitude. The choice extends a little further than this. Do I choose a helpful attitude because I have to or because I want to?

For Viktor Frankl in Dachau and Auschwitz it was a case of 'having to' summon up a positive attitude to give himself the best chance of survival. In the situation in which he found himself, those who didn't or couldn't do this simply didn't survive. In contrast to this extreme example, let's look at two more everyday examples of situations that commonly cause anxiety – the workplace and the bringing-up of young children.

In the case of bringing up young children, many of us admit only to a select group of people that we actually find this very difficult. The need to entertain them constantly, the lack of mental stimulation and the lack of time for reflection can challenge even the most committed parent. In this case, we exercise the right to choose our attitude for two compelling reasons: we do it because we want to *and* because we have to. The 'having to' is a rational decision of the head. The 'wanting to' is more likely to be an emotional decision of the heart.

The workplace, however, is somewhat different for many people. Most people try to choose a positive attitude because they *have to* even if it doesn't go much further than saying, 'I will make it through to the end of the day.' If they didn't at least go this far, those who really get little from their work would find it unbearable.

People in the 'have to' category base their choice of attitude on reason – a decision of the head. Those in the 'want to' category do so for emotional reasons – going to work and wanting to choose a positive attitude so that they can try to enjoy it too. Doing something because you have to is what propels you to do things such as going to work and bringing up children, when they perhaps don't come naturally. Choosing to do something because you want to adds an emotional edge so that you engage with your heart, too. So the question is, can you find compelling reasons to choose a positive attitude that will make you 'want' to do something? The experience will be so much more valuable as a result.

Doing a presentation because you have to do it is one thing. Getting yourself into the frame of mind where you want to do it – even though this has always been a source of anxiety for you – can help you to wish for the very circumstances that had previously caused you anxiety. Whether you do something because you have to or you want to, you are still benefiting from making a valuable choice. For the anxious reader, choosing to do nothing will mean that nothing happens. Or that things get worse.

Positive statement 2

I will try to make 'big decisions' as well as 'quick choices'.

There are two concurrent pathways we can take that will allow us to exercise our personal capacity to make choices about what we do.

Let's call the first pathway 'big decisions'. Taking this path means we decide what sort of approach to our world will make us happy. The decisions might relate, for example, to our behaviour towards others – empathy, compassion, kindness, and so on. Equally, they might relate back to ourselves, requiring us to be honest about how we contribute and what we are good at. These are choices about behaviour and they are deep ones because, if the behaviour doesn't come naturally, they will take time to become a part of us. But that investment of time is worth it. Other 'big decisions' can be things like changing jobs, moving to another environment (a different country perhaps?), or leaving a damaging relationship. These are things that fundamentally affect our lives and, if the cause of our anxiety is something major, a major decision has to be made.

We have to recognize that many of the major things that happen to us do so because of the choices we made – what job we do, where we live, and so on. We never lose the power to make choices, only our motivation to do so. Once we stop making choices, or pause to think about the results of the choices we made, we lose control of our situation.

If this is a difficult concept to grasp, or you see the disruption that making tough choices could bring, ask what could be the damage to you, your family and your friends if you spend your life in a world that doesn't suit your personal strengths?

The second pathway might be labelled 'quick choices'. These are decisions that are quick and easy to make: 'Do I need that mobile upgrade?'; 'Do I need a four-by-four when I live in the middle of the city?'; 'Do I need that new household gadget, which I will probably never use?' Once we get past the necessity question – after all, these things are fine if we really do need them – the question here is, 'Are these things adding to my level of happiness?'

Making 'quick choices' can be valuable because this allows us to make minor adjustments to current circumstances – even if it is merely to question certain actions that we make 'in the moment'. But if we make only 'quick choices', the danger is that we make only small adjustments to our life when the bigger questions need to be asked. The 'quick choices' help (and it may be all we need), but it is the 'big decisions' we make that will affect our happiness level over a lifetime.

Positive statement 3

I will choose to act.

We saw in the first chapter that it is not unusual for the anxious person to say to themselves, 'I cannot cope.' We can get ourselves into a frame of mind that says we do not have the psychological resources to deal with the thing that is causing our anxiety, or that, as Viktor Frankl says, 'Our abilities are insufficient to cope with our obligations.' But we do have a simple choice to make, and that is to recognize that change doesn't happen unless we provide the necessary energy to make it happen. The impetus to overcome the potentially damaging effects of anxiety will come from our willingness and conviction to do so.

Certainly we should never pass up the opportunity to seek the help and advice of other people who are in a position to help us. But those people cannot help us very much unless we are also able to help ourselves and make a step, even a small one, in the right direction. We cannot be nudged in the right direction if we do not want to move. The barrier to this is that we sometimes underestimate the capability we have to overcome the causes and symptoms of anxiety. But, as we saw in the first chapter, 'Who am I?' we have remarkable capabilities if only we are aware of them.

Positive statement 4

I will stay one step ahead of my anxiety.

The people who deal with anxiety best are those who are able to separate themselves from their anxieties, then view and deal with them as though they were someone else's. I hope that, having read this book, you are now able to picture yourself 'jogging alongside your anxiety' as though your anxious self is your jogging partner. You are, of course, just that small step ahead.

You should not seek to banish your anxiety: in the same way that, when you jog with a partner, you are often able to push a little more, having anxiety as your metaphorical jogging partner can sharpen your responses. What is important is that you go at the pace that suits the person you are, and that your anxiety is not running away at such a speed that you feel unable to pull it back.

Part Two – Ten quick ways to reduce anxiety and increase positivity

If, like me, you often go to the end of a book first to see what happens, I can tell you that it is an ending that you will be writing yourself. The ending can be a happy one. It is your positive approach and willingness to incorporate the seven 'C's from the introduction – and in particular to exercise 'choice' and to take 'control' – that will make it so. To help you on the way, I have reproduced here a version of a checklist I wrote for a booklet on positive thinking a few years ago. I use it myself. I hope you find it useful as a quick reference point when you need a 'nudge' in the right direction.

(1) Ask if the elephant is still in the room

Some of us have almost paralyzing anxieties that never seem to go away. They don't go away because we don't deal with them. Money problems, the wrong job, poor relationships – they can all stay with us if we don't address their causes. Don't ignore what might be uncomfortable today but which could be worse tomorrow. As in the case of the elephant (which we know is there but which everyone ignores), don't ignore your anxiety.

(2) You can always choose your attitude

You can't always choose your circumstances but you can always choose your attitude to them. The first step in dealing with anxiety is actually to choose to deal with it. It sounds obvious, but what is obvious is not always actioned.

(3) Look after your body as well as your mind

This book has been about thinking. But the healthier the body, the healthier the mind. Look after yourself physically as well as mentally.

(4) Seek pleasure and enjoyment

When anxious we drop most quickly one of the things that can get us out of anxious frames of mind – we forget that pleasure can be therapeutic. When we're anxious, having fun might come less naturally, so we sometimes have really to push ourselves to get out there and have a good time.

(5) Remind yourself you are strong

Don't dwell on your fallibilities. Emphasize the things that make you strong. Remember those 'signature strengths' from the first chapter.

(6) See yourself coming out the other side

Seeing a positive point in the future immediately helps bring you closer to it. If you are anxious it can be hard even to see that a way out is possible and you may really have to push yourself to do this. Once you have visualized that point, ask how you might get there.

(7) See other worlds

Self-absorption can be paralyzing. Try to take your thoughts away from yourself. Maintain friendships, leisure activities and the things that connect you to the outside world.

(8) Don't forget what you have done

We often underestimate what we have done. When anxious we can lose self-belief. Make a note of those successes – there are always many of them. And there will be many more.

(9) Don't forget what you can still do

I repeat the quote from the film *American Beauty*:

'It's a great thing when you find that you still have the ability to surprise yourself. It makes you wonder what else you can do.'

(10) Remember, it's never too late to start

Your future is only one second away. What is the smallest positive step you can take now to dealing with what is making you anxious? When you have decided what the step is, take that step.

And finally, now you have finished this book, you may feel tempted (and I hope you will) to say that it was a rewarding read. But the stimulation now needs to be translated into action. Why not write down the three things that have most resonated with you? Preferably three things that are based around actions you could take as a result of reading this book. Write them on a postcard, address it to yourself and ask a friend to post it to you in one month's time. It's a great way of reminding yourself that these words mean something only when they are translated into action. So when the reminder postcard arrives ask yourself – did you proactively do anything yet?

REFERENCES

I drew on the following for material relevant to this book:

BOOKS

- Albrecht, Karl, *Stress and the Manager*, Touchstone, 2002
- Bauman, Zygmunt, *Liquid Life*, Polity Books, 2003
- Brown, Mark, *The Dinosaur Strain*, ICE Books, 1993
- Bryson, Bill, *A Short History of Nearly Everything*, Doubleday, 2003
- Butler, Gillian, *Overcoming Social Anxiety and Shyness*, Robinson Publishing, 1999
- Claxton, Guy, *Hare Brain, Tortoise Mind*, Fourth Estate, 1998
- Coupland, Douglas, *Jpod*, Bloomsbury, 2006
- Dalai Lama, The, with Cutler, Harold, *The Art of Happiness at Work*, Hodder Mobius, 2005
- de Bono, Edward, *De Bono's Thinking Course*, BBC Books, 1994
- de Botton, Alain, *Status Anxiety*, Penguin Books, 2004
- De Graaf *et al.*, *Affluenza: The All-consuming Epidemic*, Berrett-Koehler, 2001
- Frankl, Viktor, *Man's Search For Meaning*, Washington Press, 1985
- Frankl, Viktor, *The Doctor and the Soul*, Souvenir Press, 1969
- Galbraith, J. K., *The Culture of Contentment*, Houghton Mifflin, 1993
- Goleman, Daniel, *Destructive Emotions*, Bloomsbury, 2000
- Goleman, Daniel, *Emotional Intelligence*, Bloomsbury, 1996
- Handy, Charles, *The Elephant and the Flea*, Hutchinson, 2001
- Handy, Charles, *Understanding Organisations*, Penguin, 1993
- Kane, Pat, *The Play Ethic*, Macmillan, 2004
- Laing, R. D., *The Mystification of Experience*, Penguin, 1967

- Lucas, Bill, and Briers, Dr Stephen, *Happy Families*, BBC Active, 2006
- Miller, Douglas, *Make Your Own Good Fortune*, BBC Active, 2006
- Miller, Douglas, *Positive Thinking, Positive Action*, BBC Active, 2005
- Seligman, Martin, *Authentic Happiness*, Nicholas Brealey, 2003
- Seligman, Martin, *Learned Optimism: How to Change Your Mind and Your Life*, Vintage Books, 2006
- Warren, Eve, and Toll, Caroline, *The Stress Workbook*, Nicholas Brealey, 1997

ARTICLES

- 'Getting Inside Your Head', *Time* magazine, 14 November 2005
- 'Modern Lover', *Guardian*, 12 November 2005
- Robert Elms article, *GQ* magazine, July 2005
- 'The Age of Rage', *The Sunday Times*, 16 July 2006
- 'Healthwatch', *Private Eye,* quoting *Daily Mail*, 18 August 2006
- 'Work until you drop: How the Long-hours Culture is Killing Us', *Guardian Online*, 20 August 2005

TELEVISION

- *Why are we so miserable?*, BBC FOUR, broadcast 15 November 2005

WEBSITES

- Readers who wish to do Martin Seligman's 'Signature Strengths' questionnaire can find it at www.authentichappiness.org
- I sourced the information, in the chapter on work, relating to email as a source of stress from the following BBC weblink: http://news.bbc.co.uk/2/hi/uk_news/654956.stm

STORIES, ANECDOTES AND EXERCISES

- I originally heard the starfish story (see page 33) told by futurologist Joel Barker, although I believe the story may have originated elsewhere.

- The 'Hot Planets' exercise (see page 16) is based on original work by Professor Mark Brown and is reproduced and adapted here with his permission.

- I would like to acknowledge the input of Chris Carling in the first chapter. Chris sends out a monthly newsletter, which can be requested via her website at www.chriscoach.com.

- I originally came across the definition of assertiveness (see page 137) in a corporate training package, *Say What You Want*, produced by Melrose Film Productions, and now distributed by Video Arts Ltd. I believe that the definition is based on original work by assertiveness experts Kate and Ken Back.

- The idea for understanding the value of exploration as a means to understanding came from Bill Bryson's fabulous book *A Short History of Nearly Everything*. If you feel like you have lost your sense of perspective, there is nothing like this book to recreate 'balance'.

- The idea for doing an eBay entry about yourself came from Douglas Coupland's book *Jpod*.

ACKNOWLEDGEMENTS

I would like to thank all of those who contributed their personal stories to this book. Personal stories are a feature in all my writings and I recognize that I asked more of people in this book than I did in my previous books on positive thinking and opportunity spotting. I thank them for giving so much of themselves. In certain cases I have changed the names of those telling us their 'stories' at their request.

My knowledge in this subject grew exponentially as I was invited to deliver over 50 workshops on work-related stress and thinking positively about work (which inevitably grew to cover 'life anxieties') for Birmingham City Council Housing Department. I am grateful to Peb Thomas, Graham Smith and Julie Hickman, Paul Wright and Hayley Deen at Wright Solutions, and the 600 or so Housing Department employees I met, for giving me the opportunity to do the most rewarding work I have ever done in a learning environment. I believe I learned as much as, if not more than, those who came to the workshops!

I would also like to thank the 50 or so people who responded to a short 'happiness' questionnaire I circulated and to those who have allowed me use some of their responses in quotation form. I am grateful to Daniela Tarizzo at UN Volunteers in Bonn for offering to circulate the questionnaire around the world and helping me to give the chapters on happiness and relationships a global perspective.

I would like to thank Emma Shackleton at BBC Active. Readers can decide whether the three books I have now written for BBC Active are good and valuable to them, but I am grateful to Emma for giving me the opportunity to do what I have imagined myself doing since about the age of ten. Josie Frame edited the book and did a fantastic job challenging the inaccuracies, the poor English and the vague observations, for which I extend my deepest thanks. Any surviving errors are of course mine. A thank you as well to Jeanette Payne for seeing the manuscript through to publication.

179